.....101 WAYS TO

stitch | craft

create

VINTAGE

QUICK & EASY PROJECTS TO MAKE FOR YOUR VINTAGE LIFESTYLE

D&C
David and Charles

www.stitchcraftcreate.co.uk

CONTENTS

INTRODUCTION

Welcome to *101 Ways to Stitch, Craft, Create Vintage*. This is a beautiful collection of vintage-inspired craft projects covering all areas of a vintage lifestyle, from fashion and food and drink to gifts and home and garden. Filled with fun and practical projects that are quick and simple to make, there is a unique craft idea for everyone wanting to embrace a vintage lifestyle.

Try your hand at creating a vintage tea stand for a tea party and then bake delicious fondant fancies to place on top. Or make a stunning vintage button bracelet for yourself or as a gift. Discover a wide range of crafts, including knitting, crochet, papercraft, sewing and cake decorating, perfect for the 'have a go crafter'.

Each project has been allocated a helpful timing and level of difficulty rating, but most projects can be created within a couple of hours, and all can easily be completed in a weekend. All of the projects are suitable for beginners.

The techniques chapter offers all of the crochet, knitting and sewing abbreviations and skills that you will need to complete the projects. Cross stitch charts are provided at the back of the book and templates for featured projects are available at: www.stitchcraftcreate.co.uk/patterns.

Use these projects as a springboard to your creativity and be inspired to stitch, craft, and create your vintage lifestyle!

FASHION

CHIC 1940s PERCHER

by Chloë Haywood, designer from Hatastic!

This 1940s-style percher is made with an upcycled felt hat brim, and created with the age of austerity in mind. Wear it when you want to feel like Celia Johnson.

YOU WILL NEED:

Old felt hat with inner circumference about 50cm (20in)

Hat elastic 30cm (12in)

Grosgrain ribbon 50cm (20in)

1. Cut the brim off the hat so the ends are cut in a diagonal. Fold the two ends together so the diagonal ends cross over, making sure that the edge of the brim folds up slightly. Sew the ends together to secure them.

2. Cut a felt oval from the left over bit of brim. This will fit in the centre to make the top of the crown.

Fold the ends of the oval inside the edges (brim) and sew in place.

3. Cut extra bits of felt into leaf shapes, and sew on to the hat to decorate and also to cover the join at the back of the hat. Sew the elastic inside the hat, to hold it in place on your head, adjusting the length to fit you comfortably.

2 HOURS

MEDIUM

FASHION

ALTERED STEEL WASHER PENDANT

by Laurel Deville

Something as ordinary as steel washers can be re-purposed into pendants
with a little magic, courtesy of vintage-style papers and jewellery.

YOU WILL NEED:

Steel washer

Coarse and fine sandpaper

Craft knife

PVA glue

Découpage sealer

Clear 3D glaze/resin

Decorative paper

Feature jewellery

Ribbon

Necklace findings

1 HOUR

EASY

1. Clean up the washer and sand with coarse sandpaper to create a roughened surface for the adhesive.

2. Draw around the washer on the back of the decorative paper, cut out the inner hole before gluing the paper on as it is very tricky to do afterwards. There is no need to cut out the main shape first. Glue the paper to the washer.

3. When the glue is dry, cut off the excess paper and lightly sand the edges with fine sandpaper. This will smooth it down so it cannot catch on anything. Seal it with a coat of découpage sealer.

4. When the sealer is dry, add a coat of Diamond Glaze or similar 3D glaze/resin. While it is wet add bits of vintage jewellery, beads and so on, and lightly press into the glaze. Leave overnight to cure. When cured attach the ribbon necklace using a lark's head knot.

VINTAGE FABRIC CORSAGE

by Kirsty Neale

This simple, machine-stitched, corsage-style brooch is made from felt with vintage fabric, ribbon and buttons, and can be easily adapted into a hair clip.

YOU WILL NEED:

Felt

Fusible web

Vintage fabric

Vintage buttons

Vintage ribbon or trim

Brooch pin

Fabric glue

2 HOURS

MEDIUM

1. Copy the flower template onto felt and cut out. Trace the four circle templates onto fusible webbing and iron each one onto the back of a piece of vintage fabric. Cut out the fabric circles, then peel away the backing paper.

2. Place the largest circle on top of the felt flower and iron into place. Add the remaining circles in the same way. Machine stitch over the top to secure, using a mixture of straight and zigzag stitch.

3. Sew two or three vintage buttons on top to decorate the front of the brooch. Cut two lengths of ribbon and glue to the back of the felt flower. Trim diagonally across the ends of each piece to stop them fraying.

4. Cut a circle of felt to cover the back of your brooch. Sew a brooch pin to the circle, roughly a third of the way down from the top edge.

5. Stick the felt circle firmly and neatly into place over the back of the brooch. Allow the glue to dry overnight before wearing.

Full-size templates for this project are available at: www.stitchcraftcreate.co.uk/patterns

FASHION

ART NOUVEAU LOBSTER CLOCHE

by Benjamin Wilson

A knitted cloche with a sequined lobster fascinator.
Vaguely Schiaparelli, and a little bit Lady Gaga.

YOU WILL NEED:

Rowan Creative Focus
Worsted 50g (1¾oz) balls:

Yarn A: 1 x ball shade 01107 (Cobalt)

Rowan Wool Cotton 4-ply
50g (1¾oz) balls:

Yarn B: 1 x ball shade 487 (Sea)

Yarn C: 1 x ball shade 492 (Aqua)

Set 4.5mm (US size 7) double
pointed needles (dpns)

4.5mm (US size 7) 40cm
(16in) circular needle

3.25mm (US size 3) straight needles

3 stitch holders

Round marker

Transparent, iridescent sequins

Pale aqua sewing thread

Toy filling

*Tension: 20sts and 24 rows = 10cm
(4in) square over stocking stitch
using 4.5mm (size 7) needles*

1 DAY

HARD

1. Hat

Using 4.5mm (US size 7) circular needle and yarn A, cast on 90sts. Place marker at end of row. With WS facing, knit every row so that the RS becomes reverse st st. Continue until the hat measures 18cm (7in) from cast on edge.

2. Decrease rounds

(Change to dpns when needed)
Rnd 1: *k2tog, k16 rep from * to end [85sts].
Rnd 2 and alt rnds: knit.
Rnd 3: *k7, sl1, k2tog, psso, k7 rep from * to end. [75sts]
Rnd 5: *k6, sl1, k2tog, psso, k6 rep from * to end. [65sts]
Rnd 7: *k5, sl1, k2tog, psso, k5 rep from * to end. [55sts]
Rnd 9: *k4, sl1, k2tog, psso, k4 rep from * to end. [45sts]
Rnd 10: *k3, sl1, k2tog, psso, k3 rep from * to end. [35sts]
Rnd 12: *k2, sl1, k2tog, psso, k2 rep from * to end. [25sts]
Rnd 14: *k1, sl1, k2tog, psso, k1 rep from * to end. [15sts]
Rnd 16: *sl1, k2tog, psso, rep from * to end. [5sts]
Thread through rem sts, secure and fasten off. Weave in ends.

3. Brim

Using 4.5mm needles, cast on 8 in A. Knit one row. Work the next 170 rows in g-st. The first row of every 10 work as follows: k1, M1, K to end.

Work 10 more rows of g-st. Bind off.

4. Short Row Shell Sections

(Make one in each size)
Using 3.25mm needles, cast on 16 (24, 30) in B. K9(13, 16). Turn work.

P3, turn work, k4, turn work, p5, turn work, k6, turn work. Continue in this way, working an extra stitch from the row below after each turn, until all stitches but one have been incorporated into the short-row shaping. Transfer onto a stitch holder.

5. Lobster Body

Cast on 18 in B.
Rnd 1, 3, 5, 7, 9: k2tog 3 times, (yo, k1) six times, k2tog 3 times
Rnd 2, 4: K.
Rnd 6, 8, 10: P.
Rnd 11: k1, k2tog, k till final 3, ssk, k1.
Rnd 12: k1, p2togtbl, p till final 3, p2tog, k1.

The next 36 rows are worked in st st with a garter stitch selvedge of 1 st at each end. The first row of every 4 should be worked as follows:

Increase rows: k1, m1, k to final st, m1, k1.

On reaching rows 8, 24, and 36 shell sections should be added as follows:

Arrange the body and shell pieces with WS facing you. Work the

selvedge st from the body piece. Next 16 (24, 30) sts, insert the needle purlwise through the next st of the shell and then through the next stitch of body. Purl both together and remove from the needle at the same time. Continue until no more shell sts remain. Work selvedge st.

After row 36, repeat rows 11 and 12 until only 6sts remain. Cast off.

6. Making up

Sew in all ends. Stretch the brim about three-quarters of the way around the hat. Attach with mattress stitch.

Use mattress stitch to seam the lobster together, stuffing as you go. The g-st selvedge will be a useful guide here. Leave the lace section un-seamed.

Using a mirror, place the lobster on the hat however pleases you. Using A, embroider French knots onto its face for eyes. Using B, freehand embroider the outline of lobster claws on the appropriate place on the hat. Fill the outline in with satin stitch and sequins. Attach sequins to the edge of the shell sections and wherever else you'd like them.

BROOMSTICK CROCHET SCARF

by Lauren Howden

Broomstick crochet is given a renaissance with this stylish wool scarf,
and it's simple to make with basic crochet skills.

YOU WILL NEED:

5mm (US size 8/H) crochet hook

25mm (US size 50) straight
knitting needle (just one!)

150g (5½oz) yarn (I used
2-ply Swaledale)

Tapestry needle

*Please note: gauge isn't important for this scarf,
so just use your favourite yarn, going up a hook
size for anything heavier than DK. Weight of
yarn required will depend on what yarn is used.
In 2-ply, I used approximately 150g (5½oz).*

2 DAYS

EASY

Please note: this project uses UK crochet terms.

1. Using the hook, chain 50 stitches.
Pull the loop of last stitch larger,
and slip it over knitting needle.
Working from left to right along
chain, insert hook into the top of
each stitch, pull a loop through and
place on needle. Continue until
there are 50 loops on needle.

2. Without turning the work, insert
the hook from right to left through
first 5 loops and slip these onto hook.

Yarn over hook and draw through the
5 loops. Ch1, then 5 dc into loops.
This twists the stitches and creates a
group. One stitch will remain on hook.

3. Insert hook into next 5 loops
on needle and slip them onto hook,
as before. Yarn over hook, draw yarn
through the 5 loops. Yarn over hook
again and pull through both the
stitches on hook. Work 4 dc into 5
loops. Repeat this step to end of loops.

4. Do not turn work. Now, treating
the 50 stitches along the top of the
groups you just created as you did the
chain in step 1, work along, pulling
50 loops onto needle. Repeat steps
until work reaches desired length.
Break the yarn, weave in ends.

*Hold the hook in your right hand and
the needle in your left, or support it
between your knees or under your arm.
Experiment with different yarn weights
to create scarves for different seasons.*

POSTAGE STAMP VINTAGE BRACELET

by Ellen Kharade

Images of vintage postage stamps can be transferred onto polymer clay
using special transfer paper to create an unusual bracelet.

YOU WILL NEED:

White polymer clay

Images of vintage postage stamps

Transfer paper suitable
for polymer clay

Antique gold beads

Beading needle

Clear varnish

Clear elastic filament

Tissue blade

Instant glue

Access to a computer,
scanner and printer

HALF A DAY

MEDIUM

1. Scan the images of the stamps
into your computer, size the images
to 2 x 2.5cm (¾ x 1in) and print onto
the shiny side of the transfer paper.
Condition white polymer clay and roll
out into a sheet of 1cm (⅜in) in depth.

2. Trim the image to size and lay it
face down onto the clay. Use the back
of a teaspoon or a burnishing tool and
gently rub over the back of the image.

3. Leave the transfer image for 30
minutes to set. Place the clay in a
shallow dish of water and agitate for
a minute or two until the backing
paper slides away. Leave the transfer
clay on a piece of kitchen towel
to dry out for about an hour.

4. Make eight transfer beads in this
way and trim to size using a tissue
blade. Using a beading needle make
two parallel holes in each of the beads,
place on a baking tray and bake for
20 minutes at 110°C (225°F). Once
cool, add a coat of clear varnish.

5. Cut two lengths of elastic
filament and thread through the
polymer clay beads followed by the
gold beads, continue until all the beads
have been threaded on. Tie the ends of
the elastic in knots and secure with a
blob of instant glue.

AUDREY MITTENS

by Claire Garland

You'll love these smart yet cosy mittens with their air of 50s
glamour and 'Audrey-Hepburn-esque' style.

YOU WILL NEED:

2 x 50g (1¾oz) balls any
pink chunky yarn – MC

For flowers: small amounts
red 4-ply yarn – MC, and
pale blue 4-ply yarn – CC

Set 5mm (US size 8) double
pointed needles (dpns)

3.25mm (US size 3) straight needles

*Please note: the flowers yarn (CC and CC1)
must be 'feltable' if you wish to felt the finished
motif – i.e. 100% pure wool, also not superwash yarn. This pattern will fit hand size 19cm
(7½in) wide (around the widest part of the
palm) by 19cm (7½in) long (from wrist to tip
of middle finger). If you wish to make a larger
pair of mittens, increase the needle size to
5.5mm or 6mm (US size 9 or 10) to adjust the
tension to 20 rows or 19 rows over 10cm (4in).*

*Tension: 18sts x 21 rows = 10cm
(4in) in stocking stitch*

1 TO 2 DAYS

HARD

1. **Stitch guide**: Mock Cable Pattern

Rnd 1: [P2, twist 2 (with working
yarn at back, k into front of 2nd
st on LH needle, stretch st just
made slightly then k into back
of first st on LH needle, sl both
sts off LH needle)] 7 times.

Rnd 2: [P2, k2] 7 times.

Rnd 3: As rnd 2.

Rnd 4: As rnd 2.

Rnd 5: As rnd 2.

2. **Yarn MC and dpns**

Cast on 28sts.

Slip 28sts p-wise over 3 dpns: N1 – 9sts,
n2 – 9sts, n3 – 10sts. Place marker
(pm) and join for working in the
rnd, being careful not to twist sts.

Rnd 1: [K2, p2] 14 times.

Work st st (knit all sts every
rnd) for next 8 rnds.

Rnds 10 – 13: Work Mock
Cable Pattern.

Divide for thumb:

Rnd 14: (inc) P2, k2, p2, kf&b, k1, m1, [p2, k2] 5 times. 30sts

Rnd 15: P2, twist 2, p2, k1, pm, k3, pm, [p2, twist 2] 5 times.

Rnd 16: (inc) P2, k2, p2, kf&b, slip marker, m1, k3, m1, slip marker, [p2, k2] 5 times. 33sts

Rnd 17: [P2, k2] twice, slip marker, k5, slip marker, [p2, k2] 5 times.

Rnd 18: (inc) [P2, k2] twice, slip marker, m1, k5, m1, slip marker, [p2, k2] 5 times. 35sts

Rnd 19: [P2, k2] twice, slip marker, k7, slip marker, [p2, k2] 5 times.

Rnd 20: (inc) [P2, twist 2] twice, slip marker, m1, k7, m1, slip marker, [p2, twist 2] 5 times. 37sts

Rnd 21: [P2, k2] twice, slip marker, k9, slip marker, [p2, k2] 5 times.

Rnd 22: (inc) [P2, k2] twice, slip marker, m1, k9, m1, slip marker, [p2, k2] 5 times. 39sts

Rnd 23: [P2, k2] twice, slip marker, k11, slide last 11 sts (the thumb stitches between the row markers) onto a length of spare yarn to rejoin later, [p2, k2] 5 times. 28sts

Rnd 24: [P2, k2] 7 times – pull the tension tight as you work above the thumb stitches.

Rnds 25–39: Work Mock Cable Pattern as set.

Please note: work extra rnds in Patt here if you want longer gloves – the following 7 rows take up about 3.5cm (1⅜in).

Work st st (knit all sts every rnd) for next 4 rnds.

Rnd 44: (dec) [K2 tog, k2] 7 times. 21sts

Rnd 45: K21.

Rnd 46: (dec) [K2 tog, k1] 7 times. 14sts

Cut yarn leaving about 20cm (8in) tail. With stitches divided equally over the needles, join for grafting.

3. **Thumb:**

Slip the 11 thumb sts off the spare yarn that is holding them and onto 2 dpns – 5sts on one, 6 on another.

Rejoin yarn pick up a stitch at hand/ thumb join, k next 11sts, pick up a stitch. 13sts

Join in the rnd.

Work st st (knit all sts every rnd) for next 3 rnds.

Rnd 4: (dec) k11, k2 tog. 12sts

Work st st (knit all sts every rnd) for next 2 rnds.

Rnd 7: (dec) Skpo, k4, k4, k2 tog. 10sts

Rnd 8: K10.

Rnd 9: (dec) K2 tog 5 times. 5sts.

Cut yarn, use the end to thread through the rem 5sts, pull up tight to close the hole, secure and weave in ends.

4. **Flower:**

Using two straight needles and yarn CC – Cast on 7sts. Cast off 6sts. *Cast on 7sts. Cast off 7sts. Rep from * 5 more times. Fasten off.

Yarn CC1 – Cast on 9sts. Cast off 8sts *Cast on 9sts. Cast off 9sts. Rep from * 4 more times. Fasten off.

Thread up the tail end. Run the threaded up needle in and put along the straight edge and pull up to bunch up the petals and join into a ring of petals. Sew CC1 petals on top of CC2 petals.

5. To felt the motif soak with fairly hot water then rub in hand soap. Wash out the soap and squeeze out the water. Rub the petals between your hands until the yarn fibres matt together. Reshape the petals whilst damp and leave to dry before sewing onto the mittens' cuffs.

VINTAGE BUTTON NECKLACE

by Samantha Horn

Vintage buttons are often a neglected part of fashion so why not make this stylish necklace with an attractive selection of them?

YOU WILL NEED:

Vintage buttons

Felt sheet

Fabric glue

Two 5mm (¼in) eyelets

Eyelet tool

Chain 40cm (16in)

Two 5mm (¼in) jump rings

Wire cutters

Pliers

Needle and thread

2 HOURS

MEDIUM

1. Lay your chosen buttons out on a piece of felt. A slightly curved shape is best to create a bib-style necklace around 10–15cm (4–6in) long. Use a good quality fabric glue to fix them in place. Leave for five to ten minutes to dry.

2. Use a needle and thread and sew each of the buttons to the felt with a couple of stitches. Carefully cut around your buttons remembering to leave a little either side of the design for the eyelets.

3. Punch a small hole in the felt either side of the design where you will attach the chain. Place the eyelet through the hole and use the eyelet tool to hammer down on the eyelet securing it. (Follow the instructions for the particular eyelet tool you are using.)

4. Using some wire cutters, cut your chain in half. Use pliers to open the jump ring and hook it through the eyelet and the last link in one half on the chain. Use the pliers

again to carefully close it so the chain is nicely secured to the felt.

5. Secure the other half of your chain with another jump ring in the same way as before. Your necklace is now ready to wear!

VINTAGE CURTAIN BAG

by Ellen Kharade

A bag made from vintage curtain material, teamed up with corduroy fabric and large chunky buttons – perfect for carrying all those essential bits and bobs.

YOU WILL NEED:

Vintage curtain fabric
32 x 32cm (12½ x 12½in)

Coordinating lining fabric
32 x 32cm (12½ x 12½in)

Blue corduroy fabric 0.25m (¼yd)

Three large chunky buttons

Blue ric rac 1m (1yd)

Selection of beads and sequins

Two wooden bag handles

Coordinating sewing threads

Sewing machine

HALF A DAY

MEDIUM

1. Pin the template for the bag to the curtain material and cut the shape out. Cut an 8 x 35cm (3⅛ x 13¾in) strip from the blue corduroy fabric, pin and machine stitch to the top of the bag. Cut a strip of blue ric rac and machine stitch across the fabric change.

2. Make the other side of the bag in the same way and decorate the floral motifs with beads and sequins. Sew three large chunky buttons across the corduroy fabric. This will be the front of the bag.

3. Cut a 3 x 12cm (1¼ x 4¾in) strip of floral fabric and fold in half. Machine stitch up the side

and thread through the handle, then machine stitch to the top of the bag. Attach the other three handle tabs in the same way.

4. With right sides facing, pin the bag sections together and machine stitch into place. Cut the lining fabric the same size as the bag shell. With right sides facing pin the lining together and machine stitch into place.

5. Turn the bag the right way and press. Turn the lining the wrong way and press down a 1.3cm (½in) hem at the raw edge. Push the lining into the bag and stitch into place using neat slip stitches.

Full-size templates for this project are available at: www.stitchcraftcreate.co.uk/patterns

FASHION

FANCY BUTTONS

by Kirsty Neale

Two ways to make vintage-inspired buttons – from shrink plastic and scanned vintage wallpaper and fabric, or from silicone putty and modelling clay.

YOU WILL NEED:

Vintage fabric or wallpaper scraps

Access to a computer,
scanner and printer

Inkjet-friendly shrink plastic

Heat gun or oven

Shape punches or dies (optional)

Hole punch

Vintage buttons

Silicone putty

Air-drying clay

Acrylic paint

Clear varnish (optional)

🕐 1 HOUR

⚙ MEDIUM

1. To make shrink-plastic buttons, scan vintage fabric or wallpaper into image-based software (e.g. Photoshop). Adjust the size, ready to print pieces roughly twice as big as each finished button. Colours will intensify on shrinking, so lighten the designs before you print, too.

2. Print the patterns onto inkjet-friendly shrink plastic and leave to dry for a few minutes. Cut or punch out shapes – you can do plain circles or something fancier if you prefer. Use a hole punch to make buttonholes in the centre of each shape.

3. Use a heat gun or the oven to heat and shrink each plastic shape. The buttonholes will also shrink as you heat. Flatten any uneven parts while the plastic is still warm by pressing down on the finished button with the base of a drinking glass.

4. To create clay buttons, press a decorative vintage button into silicone putty to make a mould. Leave the putty to cure, then remove the button. Roll some air-drying clay between the palms of your hands to soften, then push into the mould.

5. When the clay has completely hardened, pop the button out of the mould and paint in your chosen colour. Add a coat of clear varnish for an optional glossy finish.

FASHION

1950s DIRNDL SKIRT

by Lisa Fordham

Make a simple skirt design using just two lengths of fabric, gathered into a waistband, then swish about as if you're starring in your own episode of *I Love Lucy*.

YOU WILL NEED:

Vintage style cotton fabric 1.25m (1⅓yd) x 112cm (44in) wide

Zip 18cm (7in)

Two medium-sized press studs for waistband

HALF A DAY

MEDIUM

1. Lay the fabric flat on the floor and follow the template layout to cut out, in order to get the best fit with your fabric.

2. **For the waistband:** first measure your waist then add on 5cm (2in) to each side of that measurement. Measure down the length of the fabric as indicated and carefully cut your waistband out. With wrong side facing fold 1.3cm (½in) on all sides of the waistband (pin and tack if required) and iron with steam. With right sides facing fold the waistband in half lengthways and iron again. Place to one side.

3. **For the skirt:** with right sides facing join the two pieces of fabric together. Iron the seam flat. You should now have one wide piece of fabric. Fold in each side of your fabric by 3cm (1¼in) and iron again. Lay the skirt fabric flat and with thread double (and using a long length) do a running stitch along the top of the skirt. Do this twice, pulling the thread through so you have two long lengths on both sides of the fabric. Gather the fabric up.

4. Lay your gathered-up fabric on the floor. Sandwich the gathered-up skirt fabric between the waistband. Allowing for 4cm (1½in) extra waistband on each side. Ensure the gathers are evenly spaced over both sides of the skirt fabric. Open the folded waistband and, placing the skirt within the waistband, pin and tack first to the back of waistband, overlapping the skirt by about 2cm (¾in). Then fold the front of the waistband over, pin and tack all three sides together, so that the skirt is sandwiched between the waistband. Machine-stitch carefully together. Remove any pins and tacks and iron.

5. Pin, tack and sew the zip on one side of the skirt where the final opening will be. With right sides of your skirt together, pin, tack and then machine stitch your final seam together to meet the bottom of your zip. Then pin, tack and machine stitch your final zip side. (Use a zipper foot to put in your zip for a good finish.) Try your skirt on and hem appropriately – mine hangs just above the knee. Hand or machine stitch the hem. Attach two press studs to finish the waistband and press to finish.

Please note: all seams have a 2.5cm (1in) seam allowance. Seams to be finished with zigzag finishing or pinking shears if preferred (finishing seams not essential to look of skirt).

Full-size templates for this project are available at: www.stitchcraftcreate.co.uk/patterns

FASHION

VINTAGE-PRINT QUILTED MAKE-UP BAG

by Ellen Kharade

Keep all your make-up together in this pretty bag, which features vintage-style fabric and raw silk, with a quilted silk panel and yo-yo decoration.

YOU WILL NEED:

Floral cotton fabric 35 x 45cm (14 x 18in)

Jade silk 35 x 45cm (14 x 18in)

Lightweight iron-on interfacing 70 x 90cm (28 x 36in)

Wadding (batting)

Coordinating lining fabric

Yo-yo fabric 11cm (4½in) circle

Vintage button

Thin brass-toned clasp 14cm (5½in)

1 DAY

MEDIUM

1. Back floral and silk fabrics with interfacing. Pin templates for bag front, back and flap to floral fabric and cut out the pieces. Pin templates for the flap to silk and wadding and cut out. Cut a back and a front from lining fabric. Pin the wadding to the silk wrong side and tack around shape to hold together. On the front, machine stitch vertical lines 2cm (¾in) apart in a lighter thread.

2. Lay patterned flap on top of patterned bag front, wrong sides together. Mark washer position

for clasp. Make a slit in the marks through both fabrics. From right side push clasps through slits in the front piece and fold down prongs. Attach the other part of clasp to flap.

3. With right sides facing, place quilted flap and floral flap together. Machine stitch around curve. With right sides facing, pin lining pieces together and stitch around sides and base, leaving 10cm (4in) gap in base. With right sides facing,

pin floral back and front together and stitch sides and base. Pin flap to back of bag, right outside of flap against right outside of bag back. Tack all layers, with raw edges even.

4. With right sides facing insert bag into lining. Pin all thicknesses together and stitch. Turn out through opening and arrange lining. Slip stitch the gap.

5. Make a yo-yo and sew the yo-yo and button to the bag front.

Full-size templates for this project are available at: www.stitchcraftcreate.co.uk/patterns

FASHION

CREAM ROSES, RIBBON AND SPARKLE TIARA

by Angela Finch

A beautiful vintage-looking tiara using roses
and ribbon. Ideal for brides or bridesmaids.

YOU WILL NEED:

0.6mm silver-plated
copper wire 1m (1yd)

Tiara headband

Seven cream roses

Clear plastic seed rondelle
beads, about 100

Cream ribbon 1m (1yd)

Clear nail varnish

1 HOUR

EASY

1. Cut eight pieces of cream
ribbon about 10cm (4in) long.
Apply clear nail varnish to the
ends to stop them from fraying.
Wait for the varnish to dry.

2. Tie a piece of the ribbon with
a simple knot twice onto the tiara.
Attach a rose next to it using wire
to wrap around the headband.
Continue doing this until you have
used all the ribbon and roses.

3. Cut the ribbon to improve your
tiara and then reapply the nail varnish.
Wait for it to dry. The tiara is fine like
this but you can add a bit of sparkle.

4. Cut a very long piece of 0.6mm
wire and add some beads. Wrap
the wire a few times around the
tiara to anchor it and loop the wire,
each time wrapping it a few times
to anchor it. Make sure there are
enough beads to cover the loop.

5. The final loop starts from the
first ribbon and ends at the last
ribbon. Make sure you add a lot of
beads and anchor it at both ends by
wrapping the wire around the tiara.
Arrange your ribbon, roses, and wire
until you are happy with the look.

*You can make your tiara loops
bigger if desired – this will require
a little more wire and beads.*

BUNCH O' CHERRIES BROOCH
by Claire Garland

Top off your couture with a sweet and cheery cherry brooch.
For a flirty and fabulous you!

YOU WILL NEED:

Small amount red 4-ply yarn – MC

Small amount green 4-ply yarn – CC

Set 3.25mm (US size 3) double
pointed needles (dpns)

Toy filling

Brooch pin or small safety pin

Pearl beads

*Please note: yarn must be 'feltable' if you
wish to felt the finished motif – i.e., 100%
pure wool, also not superwash yarn.*

Tension: 24sts x 32
rows = 10cm (4in)

2 HOURS

EASY

1. Cherry make 2

MC – Cast on 6sts.

Rnd 1: K6.

Work as i-cord as follows:

Slide sts to other end of needle
without turning. Keeping
tension tight, pull working yarn
across the back of the i-cord.

Rnd 2: (inc) [Kf&b] 6 times. 12sts

Rnd 3: K12, knitting each set of
4sts over 3 dpns. Place marker.

With RS facing, keeping tension
fairly tight on first rnd, work
in the rnd as follows:

Rnd 4: (inc) [K1, Kf&b] 6 times. 18sts

Rnds 5, 7, 9 & 11: K.

Rnd 6: (inc) [K2, kf&b] 6 times. 24sts

Rnd 8: (inc) [K3, kf&b] 6 times. 30sts

Rnd 10: (inc) [K4, kf&b] 6 times. 36sts

Rnd 12: (dec) [K4, k2tog] 6 times. 30sts

Rnds 13, 15, 17 & 19: K.

Rnd 14: (dec) [K3, k2tog] 6 times. 24sts

Rnd 16: (dec) [K2, k2tog] 6 times. 18sts

Rnd 18: (dec) [K1, k2tog] 6 times. 12sts
Weave in the tail end. Stuff the cherry.

Rnd 20: (dec) [K2tog] 6 times. 6sts

Cut yarn, thread end through the 6sts,
pull up tight. Take the yarn through
cherry and out where you started, give
a little tug to create a dimple in top and
bottom of cherry. Secure the end.

2. Stalk and leaf make 2

CC – Leave a long tail end (to use
to sew onto the cherry) cast on
5sts, work as i-cord as before.

Cont to work as i-cord for 3cm (1¼in).

Rnd 1: (inc) Kf&b, k3, kfb. 7sts, turn
and work back and forth in rows:

Row 2: (inc) Kf&b, p5, kf&b. 9sts

Row 3: (inc) Kf&b, k7, kf&b. 11sts

Row 4: (inc) P5, k1, p5.

Row 5: (dec) K4, sl2kp, k4. 9sts

Abbreviation: sl2kp = slip 2sts, k1,
pass slipped stitches over knitted one
and off the needle to decrease 2sts.

Row 6: P4, k1, p4.

Row 7: (dec) K3, sl2kp, k3. 7sts

Row 8: P3, k1, p3.

Row 9: (dec) K2, sl2kp, k2. 5sts

Row 10: P2, k1, p2.

Row 11: (dec) K1, sl2kp, k1. 3sts

Row 12: P1, k1, p1.

Cut yarn, thread end through sts,
pull up tight and secure end.

3. Felt the cherries, leaf and stalk
by soaking in fairly hot water and rub
in hand soap. Rinse and squeeze out
the water. Rub the motif between
your hands until yarn fibres matt
together. Re-shape whilst damp.

4. When dry, sew the leaves onto
a pin of a brooch back. Embellish
with vintage pearls at will!

FAUX ENAMEL FLOWER PINS

by Kirsty Neale

This flower brooch is made from layers of shrink plastic with curved
petals to echo the look of mid-century enamel brooches.

YOU WILL NEED:

White shrink plastic

Permanent marker pens

Heat gun (or oven)

Large wooden bead

Seed beads, gems or
fancy buttons

Brooch pin

Strong glue

2 HOURS

MEDIUM

1. Use the templates to trace and
then cut out one small and one or
two large flowers from shrink plastic,
depending on whether you want to
make a two- or three-layer brooch.

2. Colour both sides of the plastic
with permanent marker pens. You can
either use a single shade, or blend two

together for a different look. Don't
worry if the ink looks streaky – this
just adds to the finished effect.

3. Take the small flower and shrink,
using a heat gun or the oven. While
the plastic is still warm, carefully
pick it up and curve the petals gently
around a large wooden bead.

4. Heat the large flower(s)
in the same way, but instead of
using a bead, shape the petals
around the smaller flower.

5. Stick the flowers together, one
inside the other. Add seed beads, a gem
or button to the centre. Glue a brooch
pin to the back of the finished flower.

Full-size templates for this project are available at: www.stitchcraftcreate.co.uk/patterns

FASHION

A TWIST ON SUFFOLK PUFFS

by Danielle Lowy

Suffolk puffs are ideal for showing off those special vintage buttons.
We're daringly turning ours into a flamboyant ring!

YOU WILL NEED:

Cotton fabric 10 x 10cm (4 x 4in)

Mug or bowl, 8cm
(3¼in) diameter

Button

Ring base

Glue gun or strong all-
purpose glue

Scissors

Needle and thread

30 MINUTES

EASY

1. Using a mug or bowl, trace an 8cm (3¼in) diameter circle on the fabric and cut it out.

2. Double thread your needle and knot the end. With the knot on the right side of the material, sew small running stitches around the circle about 5mm (¼in) in from the edge. Leave the needle threaded.

3. Pull the thread from the needle end to create a showercap-like shape. Flatten it and sew a few stitches across the centre to secure it.

4. Keeping the same needle and thread, sew the button onto the pleated side. You can sew right through to the other side of the material to make it secure. Knot and cut the thread.

5. Using a glue gun or strong liquid glue, attach the ring base to the back of the Suffolk puff. Stand back and admire!

Instead of a ring, you could add a brooch back or small hair clip, or make three Suffolk puffs and sew them to ribbon for a necklace.

FASHION

REVERSIBLE VINTAGE SHOPPING TOTE

by Annie Marston and Laura Pashby James

This simple tote bag is a great way to make use of your favourite vintage fabrics. It's reusable and reversible.

YOU WILL NEED:

Greaseproof (wax) paper

Plate to mark corner curves

Fabric for bag, two pieces of complementary vintage fabric, 0.5m (½yd) each

Ribbon, two pieces each 2m (2¼yd) long x 2.5cm (1in) wide

2 HOURS

MEDIUM

1. Create the pattern using the template and greaseproof paper. Draw a rectangle 40cm (15¾in) wide x 35cm (13¾in) high and fold in half. Use a plate to add a curve to the bottom corner. Repeat on the other side. Flip the pattern over and draw another curve. Cut out and unfold. At the top, mark a point for the straps 10cm (4in) from the side of the bag.

2. To cut out the pattern, fold the first piece of fabric (for bag outside) in half. Pin the pattern to the fabric with the bottom of the pattern in line with the fold. Cut out. Repeat with the complementary fabric (for bag lining). Press all pieces. Place the lining pieces right sides together and pin. Repeat for outside pieces of bag.

3. Sew the bag together. Start by sewing the lining pieces together with a 5mm (¼in) seam, leaving the top unsewn. Repeat for the outside pieces. Turn the outside pieces the right way out (wrong sides together). Leave the lining pieces as they are (right sides together). Place the outside of the bag within the lining of the bag (right sides together) and pin together.

4. Using the pattern as a guide, pin the straps to the bag. Leave 5cm (2in) of strap below the top edge of the bag. Ensure both straps are aligned.

Tuck the straps flat inside the bag between the right sides of the two fabrics. Sew around the top of the bag, joining the two fabrics. As you reach the straps, sew back and forth across them several times for strength. Leave a gap of 10cm (4in) unsewn.

5. Remove all pins and push the fabric through the gap, turning the bag right side out so that the right side of both fabrics is showing and the straps appear. Tuck the lining inside the bag. Slip stitch the gap closed with small stitches. Press if required.

Full-size templates for this project are available at: www.stitchcraftcreate.co.uk/patterns

HIPPY-STYLE CROCHETED SHOULDER BAG

by Lisa Fordham

Let this crocheted shoulder bag take you back to the colourful
hippy-style of the 1970s – peace and love in a bag.

YOU WILL NEED:

All yarn is DK:

1 x 100g (3½oz) of main
colour (I used purple)

1 x 20g (¾oz) pink

1 x 20g (¾oz) green

1 x 20g (¾oz) yellow

1 x 20g (¾oz) brown

1 x 20g (¾oz) blue

1 x 20g (¾oz) orange

Cotton fabric for lining 45
x 24cm (17¾ x 9½in)

Stiff card

Please note: this project uses US crochet terms.

HALF A DAY

MEDIUM

1. This bag uses simple granny squares crochet. To make a granny square first make a chain of 6 stitches. Join the chain with a sl st to make a circle. Chain 3 and work 2dc into the circle. The chain plus 2 stitches make up the first group of dc stitches. Make 1 chain, work 3dc into the ring. Ch1, work 3dc into the circle, ch1, work 3dc into the circle. The circle now has four groups of 3dc worked into it. Join with a sl st into the top of the beginning chain 3. You should now have a complete first round. Sl st across the next 2 stitches and work into the corner space. Cut the yarn and secure it. Join a new colour if desired by tying a knot into any corner space. Ch3, work 2dc, ch1, 3dc into the corner space, ch1. Work 3dc, ch1 into the next corner space, ch1 – repeat this all the way around until you come back to the start of your new colour.

Each square is worked in two contrasting colours and measures about 8 x 8cm (3 x 3in). These nine squares form the pattern on each side – a total of 18 squares.

2. Lay the crocheted squares out to form the pattern and stitch in bands of three with the main colour yarn (I used purple). Then stitch those three bands together. Repeat for the other side of bag. With right sides together, crochet round three sides using dc. Keep one side open (the top of your bag). Using dc, work your way around the top of the bag (both sides) to add three rows.

3. Make a strap by crocheting a chain of 10 stitches. Then, working across the chain, make a dc into each of the chains, turning and repeating until the strap is about 100cm (40in) long. With the bag inside out sew your strap down 2cm (¾in) from the top of the bag.

4. To make the fringe, cut a piece of 12cm (4¾in) stiff card (or however long you want your fringe to be) and loop the yarn around the card ten times. Take the looped yarn off the card. Using the natural spaces at the bottom of your bag, thread the loops through the space then open out the loops and thread one end through the other and pull down to secure. When you have done enough to fill all the spaces (I did 13 loops) pull the yarn down flat and cut the loops at the bottom.

5. Make a simple lining using a contrasting fabric. Measure your bag, then measure out a piece of fabric double the width of your bag and with 2cm (¾in) extra on the height. With right sides together, machine stitch along the bottom and side of your fabric. Fold down the top of the fabric by 2cm (¾in) and steam iron. Insert the lining bag inside the crochet bag. Secure with pins and finish by sewing the lining in place. Remove the pins and press the sewn top.

Please note: this design can also be worked in one colour – you'll need 2 x 100g (3½oz) balls of your chosen yarn.

LACE BOW BROOCH

by Mary Fogg

This vintage-inspired brooch with button detailing is made with lace,
but any lightweight fabric would work just as well.

YOU WILL NEED:

Lace or lightweight fabric
30 x 30cm (12 x 12in)

Decorative buttons

Brooch back

1 HOUR

EASY

1. Take your lace or fabric and using the templates cut out the four pieces: one measuring 24 x 11cm (9½ x 4¼in) for the main bow, two pieces each 24 x 16 x 8cm (9½ x 6¼ x 3¼in) for the hanging bow and one piece 8 x 7cm (3¼ x 2¾in) for the centre section. All seam allowances are 5mm (¼in) in the following steps.

2. Fold the piece you are using for your main bow in half lengthways with right sides together. Stitch along the top, backstitching to secure at either end. Turn the piece right side out and gently press, making sure the seam runs along the centre of the piece of fabric. Fold in half widthways.

With short ends together and the seam facing you, sew along the short end seam. Turn the piece right side out and press, making sure the short seam runs down the back centre.

3. Take the two hanging bow pieces, place right sides together, pin, and sew around the edges. Leave a gap about 5cm (2in) along the top short edge for turning. Turn right side out, poke out the corners and slip stitch the gap closed. Gently press. Take the centre piece and with right sides together, fold in half lengthways. Sew along the edge, turn back to the right side and gently press, making sure the seam runs along the centre length.

4. With the seam at the back, take the main bow piece and pinch a pleat in the centre. Hand stitch the pleat to secure. Take the centre piece, fold in half with the short ends together and the seam on the outside. Sew along the edge, turn right side out and gently press with the seam running along centre back. Pull your main bow piece through the centre piece, and then also your finished hanging bow piece at the back, making sure it hangs evenly at each side. Hand sew some stitches at the back to secure and stitch on your brooch back. Finish with some buttons for decoration.

Full-size templates for this project are available at: www.stitchcraftcreate.co.uk/patterns

FASHION

RIBBONED BUTTON BRACELET

by Danielle Lowy

Combine treasured vintage buttons with new, plain ones, to create this beautiful button bracelet.

YOU WILL NEED:

20–25 buttons, with at least 10 flat buttons

Narrow ribbon 30cm (12in)

Bracelet clasps, ideally ribbon end clasps or crimps

30 MINUTES

EASY

1. Check that your selected buttons have holes large enough for threading the ribbon through.

2. Lay all the buttons in a row in your chosen design. Any buttons with a shank (that is, a protruding piece with one hole) should be placed between flat buttons so that they sit comfortably on your wrist.

3. Thread the buttons onto the ribbon, leaving about 4cm (1½in) of ribbon at either end.

4. Check the bracelet size around your wrist, adding or removing buttons so that you have a relatively snug fit.

5. Cut the ribbon to suit your bracelet clasps. For ribbon end clasps, cut to 2cm (¾in) and affix the clasps. For bolt end rings, thread and knot the ribbons twice, then trim.

PEARLS, DIAMANTÉ AND CRYSTAL NECKLET

by Maggie Jones

An antique brooch inspired this gorgeous necklet. Made with lustrous glass pearls and pretty crystals it has a lovely, timeless quality.

YOU WILL NEED:

Diamanté brooch or pendant, with ready-made holes to attach beads

154 x 4mm (⅛in) glass pearls, ivory

25 x 6mm (¼in) glass pearls, ivory

22 x 8mm (⅜in) glass pearls, ivory

9 x 4mm (⅛in) AB clear crystal rondelles

8 x 6mm (¼in) AB clear crystal rondelles

7 x 8mm (⅜in) AB clear crystal rondelles

10 crimp beads

Nylon covered beading wire

Diamanté clasp

10 crimp covers (optional)

Flat-nosed and round-nosed pliers and flush cutters

1. If you are using a brooch and the pin is visible, you may need to remove the pin. Use pliers to do this carefully.

2. Cut a 28cm (11in) length of beading wire. Using a crimp bead, attach one end to a hole in the brooch. Thread on two 8mm (⅜in) pearls, an 8mm (⅜in) rondelle and an 8mm (⅜in) pearl. Repeat seven times then add a final pearl. Using crimp bead, attach loose end to ring of fastener.

3. Repeat above with 26cm (10¼in) wire, threading on two 6mm (¼in) pearls, a 6mm (¼in) rondelle and a 6mm (¼in) pearl. Repeat eight times then add a final pearl. Follow a third time with 24cm (9½in) wire, threading three 4mm (⅛in) pearls, a 4mm (⅛in) rondelle and a 4mm (⅛in) pearl. Repeat nine times, adding a final two pearls.

4. Cut two 30cm (12in) lengths of beading wire. Using crimp beads, attach one end of each to a hole in the brooch, on the side opposite the threaded strands. To allow the necklet to lie flat, thread 59 pearls on the outer strand and 57 on the inner. Using crimp beads, attach loose ends to the clasp fastener. If desired, use crimp covers to give a neater finish.

2 HOURS

MEDIUM

VINTAGE BUCKET HAT

by Ellen Kharade

This classic vintage-style hat was made from retro fabric – fabric popular in the 1960s or 1970s would be an ideal choice. The hat is not only easy to wear but is also easy to make.

YOU WILL NEED:

Patterned fabric 25 x
25cm (10 x 10in)

Cream lining fabric 25
x 25cm (10 x 10in)

Lightweight iron-on interfacing
25 x 25cm (10 x 10in)

Coordinating ribbon 1m (1yd)

Coordinating cotton thread

Sewing machine

HALF A DAY

EASY

1. Iron lightweight interfacing onto the back of the patterned fabric. Cut out the templates for the brim, crown and top and pin to the fabric, then cut out one of each piece. Pin the templates for the brim, crown and top to the lining fabric and cut out.

2. Pin the ribbon to the crown, centring it as you do so and then machine stitch into place. Using the patterned fabric, stitch the short ends of the crown together and press the seam open.

3. Carefully pin the right side of the crown to the right side of the top section and machine stitch into place. Take your time whilst doing this to ensure a neat finish. Open up the seam and press as before.

4. Pin the short ends of the brim together, machine stitch and press open the seam. Pin the brim to the crown of the hat, matching up the back seam and machine stitch into place. Make up the lining for the hat in exactly the same way.

5. Place the hat and lining with right sides facing, and machine stitch around the brim, leaving a 10cm (4in) gap for turning. Turn the hat the right side out through the opening and close the gap using neat stitches in coordinating thread. Make a small bow and sew to the ribbon trim.

Full-size templates for this project are available at: www.stitchcraftcreate.co.uk/patterns

FASHION

NECKTIE CUFF

by Danielle Lowy

For an original accessory, upcycle an old tie into a stylish
cuff topped off with a gorgeous vintage button.

YOU WILL NEED:

One tie

Vintage button

Medium-size popper fastener

1 HOUR

EASY

1. Cut a 27cm (10½in) length
from the wide end of the tie.
You can use more or less for
a larger or smaller wrist.

2. Sew a hem on the cut
end. Sew up the underside's
central seam if it is loose.

3. Sew one half of the popper
on the underside of the tie at the
pointed end. Sew the other half of
the popper on the top side of the tie
about 2cm (¾in) from the cut end.

4. Sew a vintage button on the top
side of the tie at the pointed end.

FASHION

VINTAGE PAPER BEAD BRACELET

by Kirsty Neale

Cylindrical beads made from vintage papers, old book pages, maps, gift wrap
and such like, can be strung into a pretty, personalized bracelet.

YOU WILL NEED:

Vintage papers

PVA glue

Cocktail stick (or toothpick)

Clear varnish

Jewellery wire

Small round beads

Pliers (optional)

1 DAY

MEDIUM

1. Copy the bead template onto
paper and cut it out. Spread a thin
layer of PVA glue over the reverse side,
as shown on the template. Starting
at the narrow end, roll the paper
around a cocktail stick. Press the sticky
wider end down firmly to secure.

2. Slide the paper bead off the
cocktail stick and leave to dry.
Make 25–30 beads in the same
way. When they're all dry, brush
on one or two coats of clear varnish
to seal and protect the paper.

3. Cut a 3m (3½yd) length of
jewellery wire. Fold it in half,
then twist a little way below the
fold to create a small loop. Slide a
round bead onto one of the wire
ends, followed by a paper bead,
and then another round bead.

4. Feed the other wire end through
the three beads in the opposite
direction. Pull both wires taut so
the paper bead sits flat and centred
below the twisted wire loop. Add
more beads in the same way.

5. When your bracelet reaches the
desired length, twist the remaining
wire ends together and snip off any
excess. Carefully bend the twisted
wire into a hook-shaped closure. Slip
this through the loop at the opposite
end to wear your finished bracelet.

Full-size templates for this project are available at: www.stitchcraftcreate.co.uk/patterns

FASHION

1940s-INSPIRED FASCINATOR

by Eloise Varin

A quick to make, elegant head piece inspired by the stylish 1940s. Why not create a few fascinators using ribbons in a variety of colours to match different outfits?

YOU WILL NEED:

Base 10cm (4in), (see step 3)

Small, curved crocodile clip

Ribbon 1.5m (1½yd) in total

Glue gun

30 MINUTES

EASY

1. Your ribbon can be one piece, or lots of differents bits of varying colours and widths. Take one piece of ribbon and straight stitch down the length of the ribbon a few millimetres (a little less than ⅛in) from one edge.

2. Once you have stitched about 10cm (4in) of ribbon, pull the thread gently so that the ribbon gathers, and repeat this step until you have used all of your ribbon.

3. Put the ribbon to one side and, using the glue gun, glue the crocodile clip to the reverse of the base. I found my base at www.thetrimmingcompany.com, but they are also available on eBay.

4. Take your gathered ribbon and arrange it on the base in a way that pleases you. Glue the ribbon using the gun. You now have a ready-to-wear fascinator!

FASHION

FOOD & DRINK

BRUSH EMBROIDERY MINI CAKE

by Ruth Clemens

Perfect as a stunning centrepiece, this little gem requires
the best vintage china you can find to serve it in style.

YOU WILL NEED:

Round mini cake 7.5cm (3in)
diameter, prepared for covering

Round cake card 13cm
(5in) diameter

Green sugarpaste (rolled fondant)

Icing (confectioners') sugar

Icing polisher

Pale green ribbon

Pearl-headed pin

Cutters: large, medium
and small blossom

Royal icing

No.2 round piping nozzle

Disposable piping bag

Paintbrush

2 HOURS

EASY

1. Roll out the green sugarpaste to
a thickness of about 4mm (⅛in) on a
surface lightly dusted with icing sugar
to prevent it from sticking. Cover the
cake with the sugarpaste, smoothing
the sides neatly with an icing polisher
and trimming the excess at the base.
Whilst the sugarpaste is still soft

imprint large, medium and small
blossoms randomly over the top and
sides of the cake. Set to one side to dry.
Cover the cake card with more of the
green sugarpaste, trimming it evenly
and imprint the blossoms again around
the outside edge. Set aside to dry.

2. Fill a piping bag fitted with a
no.2 piping nozzle with royal icing
and dampen a paintbrush with a
little water. Working on the board,
first pipe around the outline of a
blossom. Using the damp paintbrush,
brush the line of royal icing into the
centre of the flower, working all the
way around the outline, dampening
the brush again if it becomes a little

dry. Repeat around all the blossoms
on the board and set aside for the
royal icing to dry. Using the same
process work through the blossoms
imprinted onto the cake and when
finished set aside to dry completely.

3. Add a small amount of royal icing
to the centre of the board and position
the cake centrally. Trim the base of the
cake with pale green ribbon, securing
at the back with a pearl-headed pin.

4. Pipe small bulbs of royal
icing between the blossoms in
groups of three to fill any of the
larger gaps, flattening any peaks
with a damp paintbrush.

FOOD & DRINK

LEMON AND SULTANA SHORTBREAD

by *Lotte Oldfield*

These delicious and easy to make shortbread biscuits are perfect for a
classic teatime treat and would also make a great gift for a friend.

YOU WILL NEED:

125g (4½oz) butter

180g (6oz) plain
(all-purpose) flour

50g (1¾oz) golden caster
(superfine) sugar plus a
little extra for sprinkling

Zest of one lemon

20g (¾oz) sultanas
(golden raisins)

Non-stick baking sheet

1 HOUR

EASY

1. Preheat the oven to 170°C
(fan)/190°C/375°F/Gas Mark 5.
Cut the butter into cubes and beat
with the sugar in a mixing bowl
until smooth. Sift the flour in, add
the zest and sultanas and work
together until it becomes a dough.

2. Turn out onto a clean floured
surface and roll out until it is 1cm
(⅜in) thick. Cut into fingers or a
shape of your choice. Dust with
caster sugar and indent the surface
lightly with a fork, then place
on a non-stick baking sheet.

3. Chill the biscuits in a fridge
or cool place for 20 minutes and
then bake in the oven for 17 to
25 minutes, checking regularly.
Take them out when they reach a
pale golden colour and carefully
transfer onto a cooling rack.

4. Serve when cool, or
alternatively they will keep in an
airtight container for three days.

FOOD & DRINK

RUFFLE BROOCH CUPCAKES

by Fiona Pearce

These delightful cupcakes, decorated with vintage-inspired sugar ruffles
and glistening brooches, make pretty little treats for a tea party.

YOU WILL NEED:

Cupcakes baked in white paper
cases (cooled to room temperature)

Non-stick rolling pin

White flower (petal/gum) paste

Duck-egg blue and light pink
sugarpaste (rolled fondant)

Circle cutter (diameter to be the
size of the top of the cupcake)

White royal icing

Disposable piping bag

No. 2 round piping nozzle

Cocktail stick (or toothpick)

Small knife

Brooch silicone mould

Silver edible lustre dust

Fine paintbrush

Edible glue

1 HOUR

EASY

1. Using a non-stick rolling pin,
roll out some white flower paste
to about 2mm (¹⁄₁₆in) in thickness.
Use a small knife to cut out a strip
of paste 6.5cm (2⅝in) long x 3.5cm
1⅜in) wide for each cupcake. Roll
a cocktail stick along the edges of
each strip to create a ruffled effect.

2. Cover the top of each cupcake
with a 3mm (⅛in) thick circle of either
pink or duck-egg blue sugarpaste.
Attach the ruffle across the centre
of the cupcake with edible glue.
Roll out a 1cm (⅜in) wide strip
of white flower paste and attach it
along the centre of the ruffle.

3. Press a small amount of white
flower paste into a brooch mould so
that the paste is flush with the back
of the mould. Use a knife to trim
off any excess paste if necessary.

4. Flex the mould to carefully
remove the brooch. Mix some silver
edible lustre dust with water to make
a paint and apply to the surface of
the brooch using a fine paintbrush.

5. Once dry, attach the brooch to the
centre of the ruffle with royal icing.
Pipe white royal icing dots around
the edge of the cupcake using a no. 2
writer tube (round piping nozzle).

PINK BLUSH MINI CAKE

by *Ruth Clemens*

So pretty in pink, this is an elegant little cake that would be perfect to impress guests at a celebration tea.

YOU WILL NEED:

Mini cake 2.5 x 5cm (1 x 2in) square, prepared for covering

Cake card 7.5cm (3in) square

White sugarpaste (rolled fondant)

Icing (confectioners') sugar

Pink ribbon and pearl-headed pin

Flower (petal/gum) paste in white and pink

Icing polisher

Cutters: medium and small rose petal, hydrangea, small blossom

Ball tool

Foam flower pad

Pink edible lustre dust

Royal icing

No. 2 round piping nozzle

2 HOUR

MEDIUM

1. Roll out the white sugarpaste to about 4mm (⅛in) thick on a surface lightly dusted with icing sugar. Cover the cake, smoothing the sides with an icing polisher and trimming excess at the base. Cover the cake card with white sugarpaste, trimming it evenly. Set cake and card aside to dry slightly.

2. To create the rose, roll out the pink flower paste to 2mm (¹⁄₁₆in) thick. Cut out four small rose petals and two large. Transfer them to the foam flower pad and use the ball tool to thin the petal edges. Starting with a small petal, curl it around itself to form the rose centre. Wrap the remaining small petals around the centre positioning them evenly. Finish by adding the remaining large petals. Set aside to dry.

3. Roll out white flower paste and cut out four hydrangea flowers and five small blossoms. Set the hydrangea flowers into the recesses of an egg carton to dry. Take the small blossoms and fold them in quarters, so the

petals close together. Set aside to dry. Take the hydrangeas and dust the edges with pink edible lustre dust.

4. Add a small amount of royal icing to the centre of the cake card and position the cake centrally. Trim the cake base with pink ribbon, securing at the back with a pin.

5. Secure the flowers to the cake using small dots of royal icing. Position the white blossoms between the rose and hydrangeas. Pipe four small bulbs to the centre of each hydrangea and pipe bulbs of royal icing in any gaps between flowers.

BIRDCAGE CAKE POPS

by Sarah Joyce

Delicious white chocolate makes these cake pops irresistible, and the birdcage shapes
and flower decorations will complement any pretty floral china that you have.

YOU WILL NEED:

Cake pop sticks

Chocolate thermometer

Small blossom cutters

Hydrangea cutter and mould

Non-stick mat and small rolling pin

Selection of edible lustres/
blossom tints

Sugar craft paintbrush

No. 1 round piping nozzle

Piping bag

Acetate strip or baking
(parchment) paper

Cake pop mixture (or
alternatively, marzipan)

White chocolate couverture

Royal icing

White chocolate modelling paste

HALF A DAY

MEDIUM

1. Make your favourite cake pop
mixture and shape into balls or
birdcages, using around 25g (1oz) per
pop. Dip a cake pop stick into melted
white chocolate and insert into the
shapes. Leave to set for 30 minutes.

2. Temper, that is melt very gently,
200g (7oz) of white chocolate in a
small plastic bowl. Add a little dusky
pink edible blossom tint to colour the
chocolate pale pink. Dip the cake
pops into the white chocolate allowing
excess to drip back into the bowl.
Place in a cake pop holder to dry.

3. Pipe royal icing to make bars on
the birdcages. When dry paint with
edible gold lustre. Cut flowers from the

white chocolate modelling paste and
dust with shimmer-pink edible lustre.
Attach with a dot of royal icing. Pipe
small birds onto acetate using royal
icing and attach to birdcages when dry.

4. For other vintage style pops, make
hydrangeas with white chocolate
modelling paste. Vein and shape
with hydrangea mould. Dust with
shimmer-pink edible lustre and paint
the edges with gold lustre. For white
chocolate butterflies spread melted
chocolate onto acetate and add
pearl sprinkles. Cut with a butterfly
cutter before it is completely dry.

FOOD & DRINK

PINK RUFFLE FLOWER CUPCAKES

by Ruth Clemens

Ruched and ruffled, these easy-to-make cupcakes
will add a little frilly decadence to your table.

YOU WILL NEED:

6 cupcakes baked in pink paper cases

Buttercream

Pink sugarpaste (rolled fondant)

Round 6.5cm (2½in) pastry cutter

Fluted circle cutters: large,
medium and small

Paintbrush

Foam flower pad

Royal icing

No. 2 round piping nozzle

Disposable piping bag

Pearl edible lustre spray

1. Roll out the pink sugarpaste to a thickness of 3mm (⅛in) on a surface lightly dusted with icing sugar to prevent it from sticking. Cut out six circles using the 6.5cm (2½in) round cutter and set to one side to dry.

2. Roll out more of the pink sugarpaste to a depth of 3mm (⅛in) and cut out six large, fluted circles. Transfer them one at a time onto the foam flower pad and using the wrong end of paintbrush lengthways, indent a line from the outside edge into the centre, rotating the circle and working all the way around. Set the circles into

the recesses of an empty egg carton to dry. Repeat the process with six medium fluted circles and six small.

3. Once the discs and flower pieces have dried, add the royal icing to a piping bag fitted with a no. 2 nozzle. Using a small dot of royal icing secure the largest fluted circle to the centre of the plain disc. Layer on the medium and small fluted pieces, securing each with a small dot of royal icing. Add two small bulbs of royal icing to the centre of the flower. Repeat to form all the cupcake toppers.

4. Spray each of them well with pearl lustre spray. Pipe a swirl of buttercream to the top of each cupcake and place a topper centrally onto each.

1 HOUR
EASY

FOOD & DRINK

CHOCOLATE THINS

by Lotte Oldfield

A great gift to impress at a dinner party – these chocolates
look so elegant but are actually really simple to make.

YOU WILL NEED:

100g (4oz) dark (bittersweet)
chocolate (cocoa content
70% or higher)

Small pan

Heatproof bowl to fit over the pan

Baking tray (sheet)

Baking (parchment) paper

Palette knife

Your choice of toppings (see below)

1. Line the baking tray with
baking paper and have your
chosen toppings to hand. Melt the
chocolate in a heatproof bowl over
a gently simmering pan of water.
Ensure that the chocolate doesn't
burn or get any water in it.

2. Drop a teaspoon of chocolate
onto the lined baking tray. Let the
chocolate pool out into a disk – help it
with the back of the spoon if necessary.

3. If using toppings sprinkle them
on now. Top the drying chocolates
with either tiny pieces of roasted

nuts, crumbled sea salt or chilli
flakes for great flavour. Or to create
a classic vintage combination make
a batch that has half topped with
edible violet pieces and the other
half with edible rose pieces.

4. Allow to dry somewhere cool,
but avoid the fridge as this will
make the chocolate discolour.

5. Remove from the parchment with
a palette knife and serve on a vintage
plate or cake stand. If giving as a gift
these can be made a couple of days
in advance and kept in a cool place.

*For divine looking chocolates, sprinkle
when drying with a tiny piece of edible
gold leaf or edible dried petals, available
from specialist baking suppliers.*

1 HOUR

EASY

DAINTY COOKIE STACK

by Fiona Pearce

Six round fluted biscuits can be stacked in a pretty pile with royal icing and
decorated with little handmade blossoms for a vintage delicacy.

YOU WILL NEED:

Cookie dough

Fluted circle cutters: small,
medium and large (largest
cutter 7cm/2¾in in diameter)

Non-stick rolling pin

White royal icing

Disposable piping bag

No.3 round piping nozzle

White and pale pink flower
(petal/gum) paste

Small and medium blossom
plunger cutters

Ball tool

Foam mat

2 HOURS

EASY

1. To make one cookie tower, roll out
the cookie dough to approximately
5mm (¼in) in thickness and cut
out two small, two medium and
two large cookies with the fluted
circle cutters. Bake your cookies
according to the recipe and leave
them to cool completely on a
wire rack before decorating.

2. Once your cookies have cooled,
stick the same-sized cookies together
with royal icing, making three small
stacks. Cover the top of each stack
with royal icing and allow to dry.
Attach the medium-sized cookies on
top of the large cookies and the small
cookies on top of the medium ones.

3. The cookie stack will look like
a miniature three-tiered cake. It
can either be left plain, or you can
pipe a shell border in royal icing
around the edge of each tier.

4. To make assorted flowers, roll
out white and pale pink flower paste
finely using a non-stick rolling pin
on a non-stick surface. Use medium
and small blossom plunger cutters to
cut out as many flowers as desired.

5. Place the flowers onto a foam
mat then press the small end of a
ball tool into their centre to form
a 'cupped' shape. Pipe small dots
of royal icing into the centre of the
flowers and attach them to the sides
and top of the stack with royal icing.

FOOD & DRINK

TRADITIONAL TEACAKES

by Ruth Clemens

Nothing compares with a homemade fruited teacake –
it's the perfect teatime treat that has stood the test of time.

YOU WILL NEED:

Makes ten teacakes.

450g (1lb) strong white bread flour

1 tsp salt

50g (1¾oz) caster (superfine) sugar

50g (1¾oz) butter,
softened and diced

2 tsp fast-action dried yeast

100g (3½oz) raisins or
sultanas (golden raisins)

225ml (8fl oz) milk, lukewarm

50ml (2fl oz) water

2 large eggs, one beaten to glaze

2 HOURS 30 MINUTES

EASY

1. In a large bowl combine the strong white bread flour, salt, caster sugar, yeast and dried fruit. Whisk together the milk, water and egg. Make a well in the centre of the dry ingredients and add the diced softened butter, followed by the liquid. Work the ingredients together to form a rough dough.

2. Turn out onto the work surface and knead for ten minutes until the dough is soft and elastic. Place in a lightly oiled bowl, cover and set to one side for an hour to rise until doubled in size.

3. Preheat the oven to 170°C(fan)/190°C/375°F/Gas Mark 5 and prepare two baking trays by greasing well or lining with non-stick baking (parchment) paper.

4. Take the risen dough from the bowl and divide into ten equal portions. Roll each into a neat ball shape by placing your hand in a claw shape over the dough with your fingers touching the worksurface. Move your hand in a circular motion to shape the dough into a round. Flatten the ball of dough slightly with your fingertips and transfer to the baking tray, spaced well apart. Cover with a clean tea towel and allow to rise until almost doubled in size again – approximately 30 minutes.

5. Brush the top of each teacake with beaten egg and bake in the oven for 18–20 minutes until golden brown. Transfer to a wire rack to cool completely.

FOOD & DRINK

CRYSTALLIZED ROSE PETALS

by Sof McVeigh

What better way to make your summer tea party as pretty as possible with these easy to make crystallized rose petals?

YOU WILL NEED:

Fresh rose petals

1 egg white

Small bowl of caster (superfine) sugar

Small brush

Greaseproof (wax) paper

HALF A DAY

EASY

1. Take a handful of rose petals – the stronger the scent, the stronger the taste, although the flavour is always very subtle. Make sure they have not been sprayed with garden chemicals. Scatter them on a plate allowing time for any insects to hurry away. Some roses have a white part where the petal attaches to the flower head, which can be bitter to eat, so snip it out with a pair of scissors.

2. Dip your brush in the egg white and, taking one petal at a time, gently cover both sides, even trying to cover the bit where your fingers were.

3. Dip both sides of the petal in caster sugar, making sure that it is all covered. Lay it on the greaseproof paper to dry.

4. Repeat with the other petals. They take about two hours to dry. Make sure they don't stick to the paper – you may need to turn them occasionally.

You can use the petals immediately as edible decorations on cakes, or put them in an airtight jar. If left in a bowl in the open they last for one week, or for six weeks if in an airtight jar.

PURPLE AND GOLD CUPCAKES

by Ruth Clemens

Purple floral embellishments give these cupcakes a sweet and
summery look. Whisk them up for a special party guest.

YOU WILL NEED:

6 cupcakes baked in
purple paper cases

Buttercream

White and purple sugarpaste
(rolled fondant)

Icing (confectioners') sugar

Cutters: medium ivy leaf, medium
and small five-petal rose cutter

Embossing mat

Fluted circle cutter, 6.5cm
(2½in) diameter

Gold edible lustre dust

Rejuvenator fluid

Paintbrush

Royal icing

1. Roll out the white sugarpaste
to a thickness of 3mm (⅛in) on a
surface lightly dusted with icing
sugar to prevent it from sticking.
Imprint the pattern on the paste
using the embossing mat. Cut out six
circles using the 6.5cm (2½in) fluted
round cutter and set aside to dry.

2. Roll out more white sugarpaste, to
a depth of 2mm (¹⁄₁₆in) and cut out 18
ivy leaves. Set to one side.

3. From the purple sugarpaste cut
out six medium rose flowers and six
small. Set them into the recesses
of an empty egg carton to dry.

4. Mix together the gold edible
lustre dust with a little of the
rejuvenator fluid and use to paint
the ivy leaves and the centres of the
small rose flowers. Allow to dry.

5. Secure three ivy leaves to the
imprinted white disc using a little
royal icing. Set the small flower into
the medium, again securing the

two together with royal icing. Roll a
small ball of purple sugarpaste for the
centre of the flower and secure into
the centre of the petals using a light
brush of water. Fix the flower over the
ivy leaves using a small dot of royal
icing. Pipe a swirl of buttercream to
the top of each cupcake and place
a topper centrally onto each.

1 HOUR 30 MINTUES

EASY

VINTAGE BOW BISCUITS

by Fiona Pearce

Dainty bow-shaped biscuits decorated with royal icing and a pretty, edible pearl brooch. Lovely little treats for a vintage tea party.

YOU WILL NEED:

Biscuit dough

Bow biscuit template or cutter

Small knife

No. 2 round piping nozzle

Disposable piping bag

Pink food colouring

White royal icing

Squeeze bottle

Cocktail stick (or toothpick)

Edible ivory pearls

Large silver dragees (sugar balls)

HALF A DAY

EASY

1. Use a small knife to cut out the dough into the bow shape using the template as a guide. Bake the biscuits according to the recipe and then leave them to cool completely on a wire rack before decorating.

2. Prepare a batch of medium-peak royal icing and colour it with pink food colouring. Use half the royal icing to fill a disposable piping bag fitted with a no. 2 nozzle.

3. Add a few drops of water to the remaining royal icing and mix to a runny consistency. Put the runny icing into a squeeze bottle.

4. Pipe around the edge of each biscuit using the royal icing in the disposable piping bag. Fill the outlined section of each biscuit with the runny royal icing from the squeeze bottle. If required, use a cocktail stick to guide the icing to the edges.

5. Leave the biscuits to dry for at least 3–4 hours before piping details on them using the royal icing in the disposable piping bag. Create a brooch in the centre of each bow by using royal icing to stick ivory edible pearls around a large silver dragee.

Full-size templates for this project are available at: www.stitchcraftcreate.co.uk/patterns

FOOD & DRINK

EGG CUSTARD TARTS

by Ruth Clemens

Whether served as dessert or with tea, these classic tarts
bring back warm memories of nursery teatimes.

YOU WILL NEED:

Pastry

225g (8oz) plain (all-purpose) flour

100g (3½oz) butter, cold diced

75g (2¾oz) icing
(confectioners') sugar, sifted

1 egg, medium beaten

1–2 tsp cold water

Filling

200ml (7fl oz) double (heavy) cream

3 eggs, medium

65g (2½oz) caster (superfine) sugar

1 tsp vanilla extract

A little grated nutmeg

12 hole mini tart tin and paper cases

Baking beans

1 HOUR 50 MINUTES

EASY

1. To make the pastry, rub flour and
butter together. Stir in the icing sugar.
Add a beaten egg and mix. Add a little
cold water if needed. Knead to an even
consistency. Wrap in cling film (plastic
warp) and chill. Heat oven to 180°C
(fan) /200°C/400°F/Gas Mark 6.

2. Grease tin, roll out pastry and
cut 12 circles for the tin. Add a paper
case to each pastry shell and fill with
baking beans. Bake for ten minutes,
remove cases and beans and bake
for five minutes more. Remove from
oven. Reduce the oven to 120°C
(fan)/140°C/280°F/Gas Mark 1.

3. Whisk eggs and sugar in a jug.
Heat cream and vanilla in a pan to just
below boiling. Pour cream mixture
over eggs and sugar and whisk.

4. Fill pastry cases and grate nutmeg
over. Bake for 35 minutes. Cool in tin
for 15 minutes and move to a wire rack.

FOOD & DRINK

STRAWBERRY VODKA

by Lotte Oldfield

This strawberry infused vodka can be given as a gift,
drunk as a liqueur or used to flavour puddings.

YOU WILL NEED:

Large bottling jar and lid
Caster (superfine) sugar
Strawberries
Large bottle of vodka
Piece of clean muslin
Jug
Small bottling jars

1 HOUR
EASY

1. Take the large bottling jar and
ensure it is clean and sterilized
if necessary. Clean and dry the
strawberries and remove the stalks.

2. Fill the jar with the strawberries.
Tip in caster sugar until the jar is
a third full. Add vodka until the
fruit is covered. Close the bottle
and store in a cool, dark place.

3. Turn the bottle up and down
each week to mix the contents. After
a month the strawberries should be
pale and the sugar will have dissolved.
Pour off the liquid, straining it
through muslin into a clean jug.

4. Immediately fill small clean
bottles with the liqueur, which is then
ready to be used. Label the bottles.

FOOD & DRINK

FONDANT FANCIES

by Ruth Clemens

As the old saying goes, 'a little of what you fancy does you good',
and these classic dainty cakes are no exception.

YOU WILL NEED:

Makes 16 fondant fancies.

Cake

250g (9oz) butter, softened

250g (9oz) caster (superfine) sugar

4 eggs, large

250g (9oz) self-raising (-rising) flour

Zest of one lemon

2 tbsp lemon curd

250g (9oz) marzipan

Buttercream

250g (9oz) butter, softened

300g (10oz) icing
(confectioners') sugar, sifted

1 tbsp milk

800g (1lb 12oz) white
sugarpaste (rolled fondant)

50g (1¾oz) dark (bittersweet)
chocolate, melted

Cake tin 20 x 20cm (8 x 8in)

Disposable piping bag

Wire rack

Roasting tin

Food colouring

1. To make the cake, preheat the oven to 160°C(fan)/180°C/350°F/ Gas Mark 4 and line the cake tin with non-stick baking (parchment) paper. Cream together the butter and sugar until light and fluffy, add the lemon zest and mix until evenly incorporated. Beat in the eggs one at a time before folding through the flour. Add the cake mixture to the prepared tin and level roughly with the back of a spoon.

Bake in the oven for 35 minutes until golden brown and springy to the touch. Transfer the cake to a wire rack and allow to cool completely. Once cooled wrap the cake well with clingfilm (plastic wrap) and chill in the fridge for 30 minutes. Prepare the buttercream, beating together the softened butter, icing sugar and milk until light and fluffy. Set to one side.

2. Trim the edges of the chilled cake so that they are straight, and level the top using a sharp serrated knife. Spread the top of the cake with the lemon curd. On a work surface lightly dusted with icing sugar to prevent sticking, roll out the marzipan into a square large enough to cover the top of the cake. Lay the marzipan onto the top of the cake and trim the marzipan with scissors so it fits the top neatly. Using a sharp knife cut the cake into 16 equal squares.

3. Coat the sides of each mini cake with buttercream, applying it with a palette knife and smoothing as neatly as possible. Take the remaining buttercream and place it in a disposable piping bag. Pipe a small dome of the buttercream onto the marzipan on the top of each cake and place them back in the fridge to chill for 15 minutes or until the buttercream is firm.

4. To prepare the fancies for coating take a deep roasting tin and set a wire rack over the top. Work with one third of the sugarpaste at a time. Break it up into small pieces and place into a heatproof jug.

Microwave the sugarpaste on half-power level for one minute at a time, stirring frequently until the sugarpaste melts. Add in a tablespoon of water at a time until it reaches a pouring consistency. Add a little food colouring to colour the fondant to your chosen shade. Take the buttercreamed cakes from the fridge and working with a few at a time set them well spaced onto the wire rack above the roasting tin. Pour the melted fondant over the top of the fancies, pouring over enough to coat fully. As the fondant cools it will become difficult to pour, simply warm it up a little more in the microwave, stirring well before using it to coat again. Allow the coated cakes to dry before removing from the wire rack. Repeat the covering process until all the fondant fancies have been coated.

5. Melt the dark chocolate and drizzle over the top of each fondant fancy and allow to set. Transfer each to a paper case and serve.

FOOD & DRINK

GIFTS

VINTAGE CAKE STAND

by Linda Bennett

Hand craft your own vintage cake stand using vintage plates and glasses.
The plates used can be the same pattern or all different.

YOU WILL NEED:

Three plates: large,
medium and small

Two glasses, any size

Glass glue

HALF A DAY

EASY

1. Collect three different size plates in the same pattern and two matching glasses. Any odd vintage plates and glasses would also look fine – it all adds to the handmade shabby chic effect.

2. Add the glass glue to the rim of one glass. Place the glass upside down on the smallest plate.

3. Repeat with the middle-sized plate and the other glass.

4. Leave them to cure by the window, as the glass glue needs natural light to set.

5. Take the middle plate with glass attached and add more glue to the bottom of the glass. Place it in the middle of the largest plate. Repeat with the smallest plate and glass to complete.

GIFTS

PAPER CUT SILHOUETTE

by Ellen Kharade

A very personal keepsake card that will be treasured by the recipient can
be created using the Victorian technique of paper cutting.

YOU WILL NEED:

Purple cardstock

Pale blue card

Pale blue paper

Patterned blue/purple paper

Dark purple paper

Cutting mat

Scalpel and blades

Sticky pads

Spray glue

1 HOUR

EASY

1. Trace the butterfly template onto
pale blue card. Using a scalpel cut out
the shape, making the central cuts first
and then the motif outline. Change
the scalpel blade regularly to obtain
clean cuts. Turn the motif over – this
is now the front of your image.

2. Cut out a piece of purple
cardstock 17 x 28cm (6¾ x 11in) and
fold it in half. Cut out a piece of pale
blue paper 13 x 16cm (5⅛ x 6¼in)
and stick to the front of the base card.

3. Cut out a piece of patterned paper
12.5 x 15.5cm (5 x 6⅛in) and stick it to
the pale blue paper. Cover the back of
the paper cut with a fine mist of spray
adhesive and stick to a rectangle of
purple card 9.5 x 12.5cm (3¾ x 5in).

4. Stick the purple card with the
paper cut butterfly to the patterned
paper using a few sticky pads.

Full-size templates for this project are available at: www.stitchcraftcreate.co.uk/patterns

GIFTS

UPCYCLED BUBBLE MAILERS

by Lynsey Searle

Here's how to make your own stylish bubble mailers (jiffy envelopes) using vintage book pages, which are sure to delight and impress your postman!

YOU WILL NEED:

Strong paper with a vintage pattern
Bubblewrap
Double-sided adhesive tape
Adhesive tape
Paper cutter (optional)

15 MINTUES
EASY

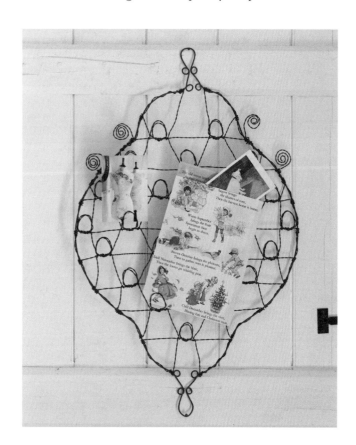

1. Take two pieces of paper (book pages or wallpaper are ideal) and ensure they are roughly the same size (any stray edges can be trimmed later). Choose which will be the front of the envelope and which will be the back. Cut 2.5cm (1in) off the top edge of the back piece.

2. Turn your back piece of paper over so that the wrong side is facing up. Add a small strip of double-sided tape around the outside edge of the paper.

3. Cut two pieces of bubble wrap that fit inside the tape, and peel the backing off the top strip of tape and stick one piece of bubble wrap to it. You may need additional tape

behind the bubblewrap, near the bottom to secure it firmly. Don't use the tape around the edges – this will be used in step 5 for securing the back of your envelope to the front.

4. Take your second piece of bubblewrap and place it on top of the other piece. Add tape to the back of the bubblewrap. Peel off all the backing and place the front of the envelope onto the top of the bubblewrap. You'll need to position it carefully but don't

worry if the edges don't match up perfectly – you can trim them later.

5. Your envelope should now look like a sandwich. Press the two pieces of paper together, using the double-sided tape positioned around the edge. The front of your envelope will be taller than the back but this extra is for your envelope flap. Stick a piece of double-sided tape onto it (peeling off the backing when you use it) or use adhesive tape.

GIFTS

VINTAGE TATTOO FLASH BROOCH

by Louise Scott

This striking embroidered felt heart brooch is based on an old school vintage tattoo flash, and would be a perfect gift for a valued friend.

YOU WILL NEED:

Red and white felt

Brooch back or safety pin

White, black and red sewing thread

Toy stuffing

2 HOURS

EASY

1. Using the templates cut out two heart-shaped pieces of red felt and one banner-shaped piece of white felt.

2. Place and pin the banner onto one of the heart shapes, and sew on using white thread.

3. Embroider your lettering onto the banner with black thread. Use a doubled strand as this makes the lettering look bolder.

4. Sew a brooch back or safety pin onto the other heart shape.

5. Sew both heart pieces together with red thread and blanket stitch. Leave a gap for the stuffing. Add the stuffing and sew up the gap.

Full-size templates for this project are available at: www.stitchcraftcreate.co.uk/patterns

GIFTS

PRETTY HAND WARMER

by Anna Wilson

This microwavable rice bag with a pretty cover is perfect for warming your hands on cold days.
It would make a thoughtful gift for an elderly relative.

YOU WILL NEED:

Patterned fabric 20 x 6cm (8 x 2⅜in)

Plain fabric 30 x 22cm (12in x 8½in)

Plain cotton 10 x 15cm (4 x 6in)

Lace 10cm (4in) long

Uncooked rice grains,
about 90g (3¼oz)

1 HOUR

MEDIUM

1. From patterned fabric cut two rectangles 10 x 6cm (4 x 2⅜in). From plain fabric cut one rectangle 10 x 6cm (4 x 2⅜in) and two more 10 x 12cm (4 x 4¾in). Cut a piece of lace 10cm (4in) long.

2. Join one of the patterned rectangles to one of the larger plain rectangles along the 10cm (4in) edge to make a larger rectangle with one patterned end. Hem the 10cm (4in)

unjoined plain edge and press. Repeat but do not hem. Hem the smaller plain rectangle along its long edge.

3. Put the two joined rectangles without hemmed edges face up. On top place the lace, the single hemmed rectangle face down and the joined pieces with hem face down. Ensure that hemmed edges face inwards and that seams match. Sew all the way round. Trim seams and turn out.

4. Cut two pieces of plain cotton 10 x 15cm (4 x 6in). Put right sides together and sew three edges. Trim seams and turn out. Fill with rice grains. Stitch the open end closed. Put the rice bag inside the cover.

5. To heat the hand warmer, remove the rice bag from the cover and microwave the rice bag for one minute.

HOME SWEET HOME KEY FOB

by Claire Garland

Make this cute house-key keeper for your home sweet home – embellish
with some favourite buttons or beads to make it truly yours.

YOU WILL NEED:

1 x 50g (1¾oz) ball cream
DK yarn – MC

Small amount green yarn – CC

Small amount blue yarn – CC1

3.5mm (US size 4) double pointed
needles (dpns) and two 3.5mm
(US size 4) circular needles

Four mismatched vintage buttons

*Tension: 24sts x 29 rows = 10cm (4in) in
stocking stitch*

3 HOURS

MEDIUM

1. In MC cast on 32sts. Use simple
sock toe to complete cast on as follows:
A. Hold needle with stitches
in left hand. Hold two empty
dpns parallel in right hand.
B. Slip 1st cast on st p-wise onto the
dpn closest to you and off needle in left
hand. Slip the next cast on st onto dpn
furthest away and off the RH needle.
Repeat step B until all stitches are
divided onto the parallel dpns,
16 sts on front dpn and 16 sts on
back. Slide sts to the other ends
of dpns, working yarn at back.
Rnd 1: Knit sts onto two
    circular needles, 16sts on
    each set. Join in the rnd.

Rnd 2: [K1, p1] 16 times.
Rnd 3: [P1, k1] 16 times.
Rep last 2 rnds seven times. Cut yarn.

2. Thread yarn needle with yarn
CC and work long stitches for
door. Sew on buttons for windows
and seed bead for doorknob.

3. Join in yarn CC1.
Rnd 16: [K2, p2] 16 times.
Rnd 17: (dec) K2 tog, [p2, k2] 3 times,
    p2 tog, [k2, p2] 3 times, k2 tog. 28sts
Rnd 18: *K1, [p2, k2] 3 times, p1*,
    rep from * to * once more.
Rnd 19: (dec) *P2 tog, p1 [k2,
    p2] twice, k1, p2 tog*, rep from
    * to * once more. 24sts
Rnd 20: (dec) K2 tog, [p2, k2]
    twice, p2 tog, p2 tog, [k2,
    p2] twice, k2 tog. 20sts
Rnd 21: *P1, [k2, k2] twice, p1*,
    rep from * to * once more.

To graft live sts tog, have needles
parallel, k front stitch tog with back
st, *k next front stitch tog with next
back st – two sts on left needle, pass
the first stitch over second needle
and off needle**, rep from * to **
twice, >k next front stitch tog with
next back st – two sts on left needle
– do not cast off>> rep from > to >>
twice. Graft and cast off (as * to **)
the last 2 sets of 3sts. Fasten off. Cut
yarn CC1. Rejoin yarn CC to 5sts.

Rnd 25: K5.
Work as i-cord for 6cm (2⅜in) as follows:
Slide sts to other end of needle
without turning. Keep gauge
tight, pull working yarn across
back of i-cord and tail ends being
concealed within i-cord. Cast off.

4. Loop cord over key ring and
sew end to source of i-cord.

VINTAGE GIFT ENVELOPE

by Amanda Stinton

A beautiful yet simple vintage inspired fabric envelope
personalized with embroidery and embellishments.

YOU WILL NEED:

For envelope 20 x 20cm
(8 x 8in) cream calico

Interfacing 20 x 20cm
(8 x 8in) (optional)

Stamps/stamping ink or fabric pens

Small scrap of fabric for stamp

Embellishments: lace, buttons,
beads and fabric scraps (optional)

Sewing machine (optional)

1 HOUR

EASY

1. Take your main fabric, calico
is ideal but linen is an alternative,
and cut out the basic envelope
shape using the template. If your
chosen fabric is quite flimsy iron
a piece of interfacing to the fabric
before cutting, to stiffen it a little.

2. Using a zigzag stitch on your
sewing machine, stitch around
all edges of the envelope shape
to prevent fraying, either in
matching or contrasting thread.
Alternatively, hem by hand.

3. Using a straight stitch sew a border
around the centre of the envelope
shape, which will become the front
of the envelope once finished. Don't
worry if your line isn't perfectly straight
as it adds to the vintage feel! This step
can be done by hand or machine.

4. Inside the border you've just
sewn you can embroider or embellish
the front of the envelope however
you want. To make the example
shown cut a small square of fabric
and sew into place as the stamp,

then use a rubber stamp and ink to
stamp a postmark and address.

5. To make the envelope, fold along
each of the flaps and press with an iron
to create a crisp fold. Fold along the
creases. Using a hand stitch sew the
two sides together where they meet
in the middle then fold the bottom
flap up and hand sew to side flaps
to complete your envelope shape.

Full-size templates for this project are available at: www.stitchcraftcreate.co.uk/patterns

GIFTS

VINTAGE BUTTON SIGNAGE

by Lucy Morris

Mismatched vintage buttons can be used to create pretty numbers or letters.
Perfect for wedding signs, birthday cards or display.

YOU WILL NEED:

Stiff cardboard

Lots of mismatched vintage buttons

Glue gun or craft glue

Craft knife

Craft board

1 HOUR

EASY

1. Decide on the letter, number or word you would like to create and draw the outline onto stiff cardboard. Use a craft knife to carefully cut out your shape or shapes. A cutting mat or chopping board is useful to protect your surfaces.

2. You can paint the card a colour of your choice, although it can look just as lovely using natural-coloured brown card.

3. Use a glue gun or strong craft adhesive to cover small areas of the card at a time and stick on the buttons. Stick them as close together as you can and in a random order until the whole surface of the card is covered. Allow to dry.

BON VOYAGE CARD

by Lotte Oldfield

A Jules Verne-inspired vintage card to wish someone well on their travels.
It's easy to change the wording for a personalized message.

YOU WILL NEED:

Ivory single fold card size A6 (4 x 6in)

Brown Kraft paper envelope,
sized to match card

Scrap of calico or similar fabric

Vintage travel image or photo

Photo corners or scrap of ivory paper

Access to computer and printer
or black transfer letters

Pinking shears

PVA or spray mount

Glue stick

1 HOUR

EASY

1. Design your message on a computer and print onto the card blank. Alternatively, draw a faint pencil line on the card and neatly add your message using transfer letters. Rub out the pencil line if necessary.

2. Cut the fabric scrap with pinking shears into a rectangle approximately 9 x 7cm (3½ x 2¾in). Press with an iron and stick with spray mount or PVA onto the card blank.

3. Find a vintage travel image, or choose a photo and turn it into sepia colours on the computer before printing it out to a size of 6 x 5cm (2⅜ x 2in). Use the glue stick to stick it centrally onto the fabric rectangle.

4. Use photo corners or make your own by cutting up a scrap of ivory card and glue to the corners of the image. This card can be easily changed to a birthday, wedding or anniversary card by adapting the message and using an old photo printed in sepia as the image.

GIFTS

PRETTY FLORAL BUNTING

by Tirke Linnemann

Beautiful multicoloured flags are perfect for wedding celebrations,
birthdays and anniversaries – or just cheering yourself up!

YOU WILL NEED:

12 different fabrics,
2m (2¼yd) in total

Bias binding 4m
(4¼yd) x 2.5cm (1in) wide

1 DAY

EASY

1. Choose your colour scheme
and select your fabrics.

2. Make a triangle template 15cm
(6in) wide x 23cm (9in) high and use it
to cut pairs of triangles from the fabrics.
Place each pair right sides together and
sew a 5mm (¼in) seam along the two
long sides. It is important to trim the
seams at the point, to get a nice sharp
point. Turn right way out, pushing out
the point with a pencil, and press.

3. Arrange your flags to balance
the fabric designs and colours. Four
flags are needed per metre (yard).

4. Sew each flag to the bias binding
by sandwiching the remaining raw
edge of the triangle in the binding,
folding the binding over the raw

edge and stitching through all
the layers. Make sure the flags are
evenly spaced as you do this.

5. Add an extra length of 50cm
(20in) of bias binding to each end
of the bunting to provide a double
ribbon and make fastening easier.

GIFTS

EMBROIDERED SEWING NEEDLE CASE

by Philippa Belcher-Love

A pretty little case to store pins and needles makes
the perfect gift for a friend who sews.

YOU WILL NEED:

Felt in two contrasting colours

Embroidery threads in
colours of your choice

Pinking shears (optional)

Pencil, paper, ruler

Transfer pen or pencil

Needles and pins

30 MINTUES

EASY

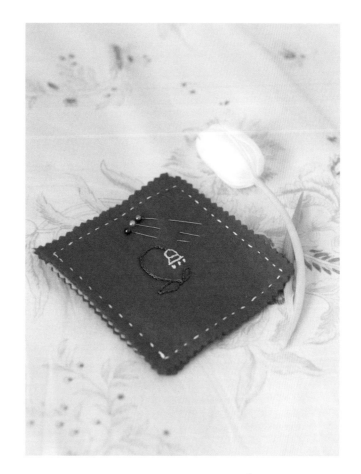

1. Cut out the template from
the felt; cut two of outer and one
of inner, in a contrast felt.

2. Trace the flower design with
transfer pen or pencil and iron on
to the centre one piece of outer
felt. Embroider over the flower
design in embroidery thread.

3. Place all pieces together,
sandwiching the inner contrasting
piece between the top embroidered
outer piece, and plain bottom
outer piece. Match the sewing
lines shown on the template.

4. Sew down the line marked
'sewing line', making sure that you
go all the way through all layers.
Continue this stitched line around the
edge of the top layer only, to create a
frame. Fill with pins and needles.

Full-size templates for this project are available at: www.stitchcraftcreate.co.uk/patterns

GIFTS

COFFEE-DYED PAPER ROSES

by Danielle Lowy

These delicate-looking paper rose ornaments are upcycled from old books, chopsticks and coffee granules! Add one to a houseplant to bring a touch of glamour.

YOU WILL NEED:

Two text-only book pages

½ tsp instant coffee granules

Sponge

Chopstick or thin piece of dowel 15cm (6in) long

Large mug

Glue gun

Thick black felt pen (optional)

30 MINTUES

EASY

1. Dissolve half a teaspoon of instant coffee into two tablespoons of warm water. Sponge onto both sides of the paper and leave to dry. Don't worry if it's a bit wrinkly, it adds to the charm.

2. Use the mug to trace a circle on the paper. Cut it into a spiral from the outside in, leaving a 2.5cm (1in) circle in the middle.

3. Starting from the outside tail, roll the paper around the end of the chopstick or dowel. Carefully remove it.

4. Put a blob of glue on the central circle and push down the centre of the rose until it sticks.

5. Make two more roses and glue gun all three to the chopstick or dowel. Experiment with different size roses or add to the vintage look by drawing the spiral in thick black felt pen for dark edges on the roses.

LOVE LINES BUNTING

by Fiona-Grace Peppler

This bespoke bunting is an ideal project to celebrate a milestone with family and friends and display precious memories.

YOU WILL NEED:

Original source material (see step 1)

Wide satin ribbon about 1m (1yd)

Other papercrafting embellishments (optional)

Paper cutting tools

Pins and quilting clips

Tape measure

Sewing machine

HALF A DAY

EASY

1. Gather your source materials – old photographs, letters, ticket stubs and other documents relating to the person or event you are celebrating. To preserve the originals, scan or copy them onto stiff paper.

2. Cut your source materials to create the bunting flags. Don't limit yourself to triangles – stars, hearts, circles or tab shapes can all work well to highlight the materials.

3. Arrange the flags to tell a story or frame the occasion. Now is also the time to make any additional flags. For instance, 'Happy Birthday' or 'Congratulations', or even narrative links between elements, such as, 'And then…' or 'Meanwhile…'.

4. Finger press and pin the ribbon in half lengthways and press for a sharp edge. Measure and mark the position of your flags with pins and fix in place

with a row of zigzag stitching. Quilting pins or hairclips make it easier to hold the flags in place while you sew.

5. Finish by hemming the ribbon. When you hang it, you can dress the hanging points with bows, or use decorative hooks or pins.

GIFTS

CROCHETED JAM JAR VOTIVE

by Anna Fazakerley

Make a pretty shade for a jam jar with this lacy crochet pattern.
The candlelight will shine through it beautifully.

YOU WILL NEED:

DK cotton yarn in your
chosen colours

Jam jar, 25cm (10in) circumference
at top x 10cm (4in) high

4mm (US size G/6) crochet hook

Yarn needle

Tea light candle

Wire and pliers (optional)

Please note: this project uses US crochet terms.

1. With main yarn colour ch35,
join in a ring to first ch, taking
care not to twist. Check the fit
over the bottom of your jar.

*(Please note, you can increase
or decrease in multiples of
five to get the perfect fit)*

Rnd 1: Ch3, dc into same ch, ch1,
2dc in same ch. *sk 4ch, 2dc,
ch1, 2dc in next ch,* repeat **
around. Sl st to top of ch3.

Rnd 2: Sl st into next st, sl st into ch sp.
Ch3, dc, ch1, 2dc in ch sp, *2dc,
ch1, 2dc in next ch sp* repeat **
around. Join to top of ch3.

Rnd 3–9: repeat round 2.
Check the fitting before starting round
10. If it seems a little short, add extra
rounds to build it up.

Rnd 10: Join edging colour. Ch1, sc
in same st. Sc in each st and in each
space around. Join to top of first sc.

Rnd 11: *Ch3, sk 1sc, sl st in
next st,* repeat ** to end.
Fasten off. Sew in ends.

2. Slide the finished sleeve over
your jar. Place the tea light inside
to light up the jar. It will cast pretty
shadows against surfaces and walls and
create a soft light in the evenings.

3. You can add a wire carry handle
to turn this into a lantern. Bend a
length of wire into a handle shape
and loop each end through the
crocheted edging either side, twisting
it back on itself to hold in place.

1 HOUR

EASY

SPOTTY DOG BANDANA

by Lotte Oldfield

Dress your dog with a difference. Use paisley, spots or floral fabrics
to lend the bandana that vintage look.

YOU WILL NEED:

Tape measure
Spotty fabric
Pinking shears
Coordinating fabric
Sewing machine

1. Loosely measure around the base of your dog's neck. Add 30cm (12in) to this measurement and make a note of it. Enlarge or reduce the template until the long edge is the measurement you have noted down. Print out.

2. Place your template on your clean, pressed fabric, so that the long edge is on the bias of the fabric. Pin and cut out with pinking shears. Remove pins and template.

3. Turn over 1.3cm (½in) on all edges. Pin and press. Stitch this hem with zigzag stitch in a coordinating thread. Trim off any loose threads.

4. Loosely wrap around the very base of your dog's neck and tie the two pointed ends into a knot. Adjust the fabric around the knot until all the reverse of the fabric is hidden. Ensure the bandana is a loose fit and not too tight.

5. If the ends of the knot look too long you can trim the very points of the ends off with pinking shears near to the hem. The bandana is for show only and should not be used instead of a collar or with a lead.

1 HOUR
EASY

Full-size templates for this project are available at: www.stitchcraftcreate.co.uk/patterns

GIFTS

NEW HOME CARD

by Jeni Hennah

Cross stitch four vintage-style keys on a recycled
card to welcome a friend to a new home.

YOU WILL NEED:

13 x 13cm (5 x 5in) recycled
single-fold card

Patterned paper or card

White 28-count linen (or 14-count
Aida), 5.5 x 5cm (2¼ x 2in)

Dark grey stranded cotton (floss)

Glue or double-sided tape

1 HOUR

EASY

1. Take the linen (or Aida) and
mark the centre. Use the centre
point as a guide to position
the cross stitch design.

2. Cross stitch the design with
two strands of dark grey stranded
cotton following the chart provided
at the end of this book.

3. Carefully cut an aperture in the
centre of the front of your card blank.
To work out the size of your aperture,
measure your finished cross stitch
and add about 5mm (¼in) to each
side. If you've used 28-count linen or
14-count Aida, your aperture should
be about 5 x 4.5cm (2¼ x 1¾in), which
will house the embroidery nicely.

4. Attach the cross-stitched
piece to the inside of the card
with glue or double-sided tape.

5. Cut a piece of patterned paper
or card slightly smaller than your
card blank and stick this on the
inside front of the card to cover
the back of the cross stitch.

The cross stitch chart for this project is available at the back of the book and at: www.stitchcraftcreate.co.uk/patterns

GIFTS

APPLIQUÉD AND EMBROIDERED PINCUSHION

by Linda Clements

This charming pincushion is ideal as a gift for a friend. Decorate it with appliqué, hand embroidery and small embellishments, such as tiny buttons and lace motifs.

YOU WILL NEED:

Linen two 9cm (3½in) squares

Print for border: four pieces 4.4 x 9cm (1¾ x 3½in) and four 4.4 x 15.2cm (1¾ x 6in)

Scraps of print fabrics for appliqué

Fusible web

Embellishments of your choice

Stranded cotton (floss) in colours to suit your fabrics

Toy stuffing

3 HOURS

EASY

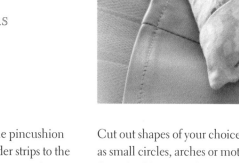

1. Make the front of the pincushion by sewing the short border strips to the sides of the linen square, using 6mm (¼in) seams. Press the seams and then sew the longer strips to the top and bottom and press. Prepare the back of the pincushion in the same way.

2. Decorate the front of the pincushion by first backing your print fabrics with fusible web.

Cut out shapes of your choice, such as small circles, arches or motifs from the fabric and fuse these to the linen. Edge the appliqués with blanket stitch or whip stitch.

3. Sew on tiny buttons, little lace motifs and metallic charms and then add some hand embroidery as desired to further embellish the pincushion. Decorate the back too if you like.

4. Place the two pieces right sides together and sew together all round, leaving a gap for turning through. Turn through, press the seam and then stuff well with toy stuffing. Turn the gap under and sew up with matching thread.

FRILLY BABY HAT

by Lauraine Wishart

This beautiful vintage-inspired baby hat is ideal as a gift for a special occasion, such as a first birthday or a christening.

YOU WILL NEED:

1 x 50g (1¾oz) ball of double knit wool

Beads

Faux fur

4mm (US size G/6) needles

HALF A DAY

MEDIUM

1. Cast on 75sts.

Row 1: *P3, k1, p1 then knit 1 into the next stitch – repeat from * to end
Row 2, 4 & 6: *K3, p3 and repeat from * to end.

2. **Row 3**: *P3, k1, then pick 1st up from row below, k1 then pick 1st up from row below, k1 – repeat from * to end.

3. **Row 5**: *P3, k1, then pick 1st up from row below, k3 then pick 1st up from row below, k1 – repeat from * to end.
Row 7: P3, *cast off 7sts, p2 repeat from * to last 3sts, p3.

4. **Row 8**: K3, *cast on 1st k2, repeat from * to last 3sts, k3.

Knit 12 rows stocking stitch then repeat the last 8 rows again.
Knit 4 rows stocking stitch.
Next row: K.
Next row: *K1, yfwd, k2tog, repeat from * to end.

5. **Next row**: K and then work 6 rows in stocking stitch.
Next row: *K1, yfwd, k2tog, repeat from * to end.
Starting with a purl row, work 5 rows of stocking stitch.

6. **Next row**: Pick up the stitch from the first row of the 6 knitted rows below the hole rows and knit this with the next stitch, repeating all the way to the end to make the picot.
Next row: K.
Shape the crown as follows:

K4 *slip 1, k2tog, psso, k7, repeat from * to end.
Starting with a purl row, stocking stitch the next 3 rows.
K3, *slip 1, k2tog, psso, k5 repeat from * to end.
Starting with a purl row, stocking stitch the next 3 rows.
K2*slip 1, k2tog, psso, k3, repeat from * to end.
Next row: P.
K1*slip 1, k2tog, psso, k1, repeat from * to end.

7. Break the wool and thread through the remaining stitches and sew the crown area. Decorate as desired with the fur and beads.

GORGEOUS GIFT BOX

by Danielle Lowy

Give new life to a pretty birthday card with this little gift box, perhaps
for a handmade item of jewellery or a little posy of flowers.

YOU WILL NEED:

Greetings card 12cm (4¾in) wide

Ruler

Glue

Paperclips

Small piece of tissue paper

30 MINTUES

EASY

1. Cut the card in half at the spine. Snip off a 2mm (¹⁄₁₆in) strip from the top and one side of the back of the card – this will be the bottom of the box and the front of the card will be the top.

2. Now follow the same instructions for both pieces of card. On the wrong side of the card, measure 3cm (1¼in) margins from the edges along all four sides of the card. Score along the lines and fold them inwards.

3. At each corner there is now a square. Cut a tab on the inside of the squares up to the 3cm (1¼in) line at the top and bottom of the card. That is, make four cuts on each card.

4. Glue the tabs and fold the card to make a box shape. Hold the tabs in place with paperclips until dry.

5. Fold some tissue paper for the inside of the box.

GIFTS

PERSONALIZED WINE CRATE

by Lotte Oldfield

This bespoke box can be filled with wine to lay down as a future
birthday or anniversary present for someone special.

YOU WILL NEED:

Wooden wine box

Good bottle of wine

Packing material (optional)

Ruler

Access to a computer and printer

Printer paper

A4 (letter size) card

Cutting mat

Craft knife

Spray mount

Newspaper

Spray paint

Luggage or gift label

1. Measure crate lid and side. On a computer, create two documents, one with the dimensions of the lid the other dimensions of the side. Type out two designs in a very bold font: one of the date of the celebration or anniversary and the other of the recipient's initials.

2. Print out each document and stick to a piece of card. Trim down to the document size. Cut out the letters carefully on a cutting mat with a craft knife to make a stencil. Lightly spray the reverse with spray mount to give it a slightly tacky surface when dry.

3. Ensure that the wine crate is clean and dry. On newspaper in an outdoor area, place the initials stencil on the lid of the crate, making sure it is centred and all edges have good contact with the wood. Mask off the surround area with newspaper.

4. Following the directions and safety instructions on the spray paint, give the stencil a light, even coating of paint holding the paint can at a 90-degree angle to the area you are spraying. Take care not to spray under the edges of the letters. Leave to dry and repeat this process.

5. Remove the stencil only when dry. Repeat the spraying process with the date stencil on both sides of the crate. Fill the crate with the wine and packing material (raffia or tissue paper), if needed. Make a label for the recipient letting them know when the wine should be drunk.

2 HOURS

HARD

GENTLEMAN'S NOTEBOOK

by Jeni Hennah

A felt notebook cover with cross-stitched bowler hat, moustache
and cane motifs, for the dapper gent with lists to make.

YOU WILL NEED:

White 28-count linen,
5.5 x 5cm (2¼ x 2in)

Dark brown felt

Dark brown or black
stranded cotton (floss)

Notebook

HALF A DAY

MEDIUM

*Please note that this design includes half
cross stitches, so linen is recommended.*

1. Take the piece of linen and mark
the centre. Use the centre point as
a guide for positioning the design.

2. Cross stitch the design using
two strands of black or dark brown
stranded cotton following the chart
provided at the end of this book.

3. Measure the height and width
of the front cover of your notebook
and the width of the spine. Double
the measurement for the width of the
front cover (to allow for the back cover)
and then add the spine width. This
is the total width of your notebook.

To calculate the size of the felt strip
needed for your cover add 1.3cm
(½in) to the height and 10cm (4in) to
the total width. The notebook shown
here has a height of 12cm (4¾in) with
a front cover width of 16cm (6¼in)
and a spine width of 0.5cm (¼in), so
the felt strip would be 13.3 x 42.5cm
(5¼ x 16¾in). Cut a piece of dark
brown felt to the required size.

4. Fold over each side of the felt strip
in by 5cm (2in) and sew all around
the edges to hold in place. Attach the
cross-stitched piece to the front of the
felt piece with blanket stitch using two
strands of dark brown stranded cotton.

5. Wrap the felt piece around the
notebook by pushing the book cover
into the flaps at the front and back.

The cross stitch chart for this project is available at the back of the book and at: www.stitchcraftcreate.co.uk/patterns

GIFTS

CUTE VINTAGE COIN PURSE

by Claire Garland

This pretty little coin purse with its peachy
bloom will brighten your halcyon days.

YOU WILL NEED:

Half a 50g (1¾oz) ball of
cream DK yarn – MC

Lengths 4-ply or crewel wool (used
double) to match charted motif

Vintage fabric 46 x 55cm (18 x 22in)

4.5mm (US size 7) knitting needles

Tapestry needle

Purse frame 10 x 5cm (4 x 2in)

Suitable glue

*Tension: 21sts x 28 rows = 10cm
(4in) in stocking stitch*

3 HOURS

MEDIUM

1. **Front then back of purse**
Cast on 22sts. Beg with a k row, work
15 rows st st. Place marker at each end
of next row to mark 'Hinge Point'.
Row 16: Kf&b, p20, kf&b. 24sts
St st 2 rows.
Row 19: K1, m1, k to last st, m1, k1.
26sts
Row 20: Kf&b, p to last st, kf&b. 28sts
Row 21: K14, place marker on last
stitch to mark beg of motif (red dot
on chart). St st 9 rows.
Row 31: K2 tog, k to last 2 sts, k2 tog.
Row 32: P1, p2 tog, p to last
3sts, p2 tog, p1. 24sts
St st 2 rows.

Place marker at each end of next row
to mark 'Hinge Point'.
Row 35: Skpo, k20, k2 tog. 22sts.
St st 15 rows. Cast off. Press flat.

2. Cross stitch the motif,
beginning at red dot on chart.

3. Using purse frame and knitted
panel, make template to cut lining,
marking hinge markers and allowing
1cm (⅜in) seam around sides and top
edges. Cut lining piece. Fold knitted
panel in half, right sides together.
Backstitch side seams from hinge
point down both sides. Turn out.

Fold the fabric panel in half, with
right sides together. Sew side seams
from the hinge point down both
sides. Press the seam allowance from
hinge and top edge on fabric panel
to wrong sides. Tack lining the inside
the purse, wrong sides together.

4. Apply glue to one side of the frame
and to top and side edges of fabric
around one side of opening. Insert
one side of purse into frame, starting
at the hinge. Check lining is even.
Allow to dry. Repeat on the other side.

The cross stitch chart for this project is available at the back of the book and at: www.stitchcraftcreate.co.uk/patterns

GIFTS

CROCHETED TEA SET

by Anna Fazakerley

This adorably pretty and cuddly crochet teapot, cups and saucers is perfect for a child's play set – or just for fun!

YOU WILL NEED:

DK acrylic yarn: white, pink, blue, green and gold

Toy stuffing

3.5mm (US size E/4) crochet hook

Yarn needle

Spray starch (optional)

1 DAY

HARD

Please note: this project uses US crochet terms.

1. Tea circle for cup

Rnd 1: Ch4, 13dc in 4th ch from hook. Join with a sl st to top of ch4. (14 dc)

Rnd 2: Ch2, hdc in same st, 2hdc in each st around. Join with a sl st to top of ch2. Fasten off. (28 hdc)

2. Teacup

Rnd 1: Ch4, 11dc in 4th ch from hook, join with a sl st to 4th ch of beginning ch4. (12dc)

Rnd 2: Ch2, hdc in same st, 2hdc in next 11 st, join to top of beg ch2. (24 hdc)

Rnd 3: *Working in back loops only:* Ch1, sc in each st around, join to top of 1st sc. (24 blsc)

Rnd 4: *Working through all loops:* Ch2, hdc in next 5st, *2hdc in next st, hdc in next 5st* repeat between **, join to top of beg ch2. (28hdc)

Rnd 5: Ch2, hdc in same st, hdc in next st and each remaining st. Join to top of beg ch2. (28hdc)

Rnd 6: Repeat round 5.

Rnd 7: Attach tea circle. Ch1, turn. *(Position tea circle inside the rim and hold so that the outer stitches are level with the top of round 6 with rs facing upwards.)* Sc into back loops of tea circle and facing 1st st of round 6 to join the two edges together, repeat around and join with sl st to beg sc. *(Stuff the cavity when you are a few stitches from the end.)*

Rnd 8: Ch1, sc in same st, sc in each st around. Join with sl st to first sc. Fasten off.

Rnd 9: *Join yarn to base of cup in the front loops of round 3.* Ch1, sc in same st and in each st around. Join with a sl st to 1st sc. Fasten off and sew in end.

Rnd 10: *Join gold yarn to the top of the cup in round 8.* Ch1, sc same st, sc in each st around, join to 1st sc with a sl st. Fasten off and stitch in end.

3. Handle

Row 1: *Working in rows:* Ch9 then turn and sc in second ch from hook and in each ch along. (8sc)

Row 2: C1, turn, sc in same st as ch1 and in each st along. (8sc)

Row 3: Repeat row 2. Fasten off leaving a long tail.

Position the strip against the side of the cup where the handle would sit. Stitch the bottom of the strip near the base of the cup, then roll the strip into a tube and oversew the edges together on the inside. Stitch the open end of the strip near the rim.

4. Flower and leaf decoration

Flower

Rnd 1: Using the flower colour ch2, 6sc into 2nd ch from hook then join with a sl st to beg sc.

Rnd 2: Ch2, 2hdc in same st, sl st in next st, *3hdc in next st, sl st in next st,* repeat between ** once more. Join with sl st to top of ch2. Fasten off leaving a long tail.

Leaf

Rnd 1: Ch3, hdc in 2nd ch from hook, sl st in last ch. Fasten off leaving a tail then stitch onto flower.

Attach the flower to cup by stitching on with long tail. Hide yarn in cup body.

5. Saucer

Rnd 1: Ch4, 11dc in 4th ch from hook, join with a sl st to 4th ch of beginning ch4. (12dc)

Rnd 2: Ch2, hdc in same st, 2hdc in next 11st, join to top of beg ch2. (24 hdc)

Rnd 3: *Working in front loops only:* Ch1, sc in same st, sc in each st around. Join with a sl st to top of first sc.

Rnd 4: Ch2, hdc in same st, 2hdc in each st around. Join with a sl st to top of ch2. (48hdc)

Rnd 5: Ch2, hdc in next st, hdc in each st around. Join with a sl st to top of ch2. Fasten off.

Rnd 6: *Join gold yarn to edge of saucer.* Ch1, sc in same st, sc in each st around, join with a sl st to first sc. Fasten off and sew in all loose ends.

6. Tea circle for teapot

Rnd 1: 4ch, 11dc in 4th ch from hook. Join to top of ch4. (12dc)

Rnd 2: Ch3, dc in same st, 2dc in each st. Join to top of ch3. (24dc)

7. Teapot

Rnd 1: Ch4, 11dc in 4th ch from hook, join with a sl st to 4th ch of beginning ch4. (12dc)

Rnd 2: Ch2, hdc in same st, 2hdc in next 11st, join to top of beg ch2. (24 hdc)

Rnd 3: *Working in back loops only:* Ch1, sc in each st around, join to top of 1st sc. (24 blsc)

Rnd 4: Ch2, hdc in same st, hdc in next st, *2hdc in next st, hdc in next st*, repeat between ** around. Join with a sl st to top of ch2. (36hdc)

Rnd 5: Repeat round 4. (54hdc)

Rnd 6: Ch2, hdc in next st and in each st around. Join to top of ch2.

Rnd 7–8: Repeat round 6.

Rnd 9: Ch2, hdc in next st and in each st around up to last 8 stitches. Ch8, sk last 8st, join with a sl st to top of ch2.

Rnd 10: Ch1, turn, sc in same st, sc in each missed st of round 9, sc in post of previous hdc, sc in each ch, sc in post of hdc, Sl st into 1st sc. (18sc) *(this will make the base of the spout)*

Rnd 11: Ch1, sc into same st, sc in each st around. Join to 1st sc.

Rnd 12: Ch2, hdc in next st and each st around. Join to top of ch2.

Rnd 13: Ch2, hdc two st together, *hdc in next st, hdc two st together,* around. Join to top of ch2. (12hdc)

Rnd 14: Repeat round 13. (8hdc)

Rnd 15: Ch2, hdc in next and each st. Join to top of ch2.

Rnd 16: Repeat round 15.

Rnd 17: Ch3, dc in next 3st, sc in next 4st, sl st top top of ch3. Fasten off.

Rnd 18: *Join yarn to the left of the base of the spout, back in round 9.* Ch2, hdc in next st and each st around, working through the bottom of the stitches of the spout when you get to it. Join at top of ch2. (54hdc)

Rnd 19: Ch2, hdc in next st and each st around. Join to top of ch2. (54hdc)

Rnd 20: Ch2, hdc 2st together, *hdc in next st, hdc 2st together,* repeat ** around. Join to ch2. (36hdc)

Rnd 21: Ch2, hdc in next st and each st around. (36hdc)

Rnd 22: Repeat round 20. (24hdc)

Rnd 23: *Attach tea circle. Ch1, turn. (Position tea circle inside the rim and hold so that the outer stitches are level with the top of round 22 with rs facing upwards.)* Sc into back loops of tea circle and facing 1st st of round 6, to join the two edges together, repeat around and join with sl st to beg sc. *(Stuff the cavity and spout when you are a few stitches from the end.)*

Rnd 24: Turn, Ch3, 4dc in same st, sk next st, *sl st into next st, sk next st, 5dc into next st, sk next st* repeat between ** around, join with sl st to top of ch3. Fasten off (5 5dc fans, 6 sl st)

Rnd 25: *Join yarn to base of teapot in the front loops of round 3. Ch1, sc in same st and in each st around. Join with a sl st to 1st sc. Fasten off and sew in end.*

Rnd 26: *Join gold yarn to top of pot in round 24. Ch1, sc in same st and in each st around. Join with sl st to beg sc. Fasten off and sew in tail.*

Using some white yarn, sew the base of the spout into place against the side of the teapot as shown in the picture. This gives a more realistic shape.

8. Handle

Row 1: Ch15, sc in 2nd ch from hook, sc in each st along. (14sc)

Row 2: Turn, ch1, sc same st, sc each st along.

Rows 3-6: Repeat row 2. Fasten off leaving a long tail. *(Sew the handle on, as with the teacup.)*

9. Lid

Rnd 1: Ch4, 11dc in 4th ch from hook. Join to top of ch4. (12dc)

Rnd 2: Ch3, dc in same st, 2dc in each st. Join to top of ch3 (24dc)

Rnd 3: *Working in back loops only:* Ch1, sc in each st around, join to top of 1st sc. (24 blsc)

Rnd 4: Ch2, hdc 2 st together, *hdc, hdc 2 st together,* repeat ** around. Join to top of ch2. Fasten off. (16hdc)

Rnd 5: *Join gold to front loops of round 3. Ch1, sc in same st and each st around. Join to 1st sc. Fasten off.*

Handle of lid

Rnd 1: Ch2, 6sc in 2nd ch from hook. Join to 1st sc. (6sc)

Rnd 2: Ch1, sc same st, 2sc in next st, *sc next st, 2sc in next st,* repeat ** around. Join to 1st sc. (9sc)

Rnd 3: Ch1, sc in same st and in each st around. (9sc)

Rnd 4: Repeat round 3.

Rnd 5: Ch1, sc same st, sc2together, *sc next st, sc2together*, repeat ** around. Join to 1st sc. (6sc)

Stuff and stitch to top of lid.

10. Flower decoration

Rnd 1: Ch5, dc in 5th ch from hook, ch1, *dc in same ch, ch1* repeat ** twice, join to ch4 of beg ch. (5dc, ch1)

Rnd 2: Sl st into ch1 sp. ch2, 2hdc in same sp, sl st next st, *3hdc in next ch1 sp, sl st in next st*, repeat ** around. Join to top of ch2. Fasten off leaving a long tail.

11. Leaf

Rnd 1: Ch5, hdc in 3rd ch from hook, hdc in next ch, sl st in last ch. fasten off. Stitch to flower.

Make as many flowers and leaves as you like to decorate. I used a combination of large flowers as above, with smaller flowers like the teacup ones. You could choose to embroider flowers and details instead if you prefer.

If you have made these items as cute little decorations rather than toys, help them keep their shape with a little spray starch.

FELT POM POMS

by Lotte Oldfield

Colourful, tactile decorations that can be hung alone or turned into a
baby mobile, table centrepieces or Christmas decorations.

YOU WILL NEED:

Felt

Ribbon or thread

Circular object to draw around

Needle and thread or
a hot glue gun

1. Mark out nine circles on the felt. Use a bowl or something circular to draw around. The size of the template will be the size of your finished pom pom. Cut out the circles within the line so that the pen doesn't show.

2. Fold the first circle in quarter. Make a couple of stitches at the bottom corner to secure it into its folded cone shape. Alternatively, use a dot of hot glue from a glue gun to secure. Repeat with all but one of the circles.

3. On the final circle stitch or glue your thread or ribbon to the centre before folding in quarter. Secure like the others with two stitches or glue. This will be the hanging for your pom pom.

4. Take a folded section and stitch or glue the pointed end to another section. Repeat this until you have formed all the sections into a ball shape. Fluff up the ball and your pom pom is finished.

5. Alternatively, you can make pom poms that sit on top of dowel sticks. Glue a piece of wooden dowel to the centre instead of the ribbon or thread described in step 3, then continue the project as in step 4.

1 HOUR

EASY

GIFTS

PAPER URN

by Danielle Lowy

This strong but delicate-looking urn is perfect as a dressing table
jewellery holder or for storing craft accessories.

YOU WILL NEED:

35 pages from a small text-only
book, 20 x 12cm (8 x 4¾in)

Glue stick

PVA glue

½ tsp instant coffee

Paintbrush

Double-sided adhesive
tape or glue gun

HALF A DAY

MEDIUM

1. Cut all book pages in half
lengthwise so you have 70 sheets
about 20 x 6cm (8 x 2⅜in). Fold each
sheet twice horizontally, so you have
strips about 20 x 1.5cm (8 x ⅝in).

2. Roll a strip into a tight spiral
and glue the end with the glue stick.
Glue one end of another strip and
add it to the spiral. Don't glue the
entire length of the paper, only the
beginning and end of the strips.
Add all but two of the strips.

3. Starting from the outside
layers of the spiral, pull up gently to
create the pot. Be careful not to pull
beyond the width of the strips or it
will unravel. Take your time here
to create your desired urn shape.

4. Make a handle by rolling a
strip three-quarters of its length one
way. Glue it in place. Turn the strip
over, roll the remaining quarter
strip and glue it down. Make a
second handle. Set to one side.

5. Dilute the coffee in a tablespoon
of warm water and mix into
undiluted PVA glue. Brush inside
and outside the urn. Leave to dry
and re-apply twice. Do the same
with the handles. When all are dry,
secure the handles to the urn with
double-sided tape or a glue gun.

GIFTS

HOME & GARDEN

VINTAGE FRAME NOTICEBOARD

by Kirsty Neale

This decorative pinboard can be created from an old picture frame, with the glass removed and cork tiles or vintage fabric added in its place.

YOU WILL NEED:

Vintage picture frame

Sandpaper

Spray paint or acrylic paint and paintbrush

Adhesive cork or cork tiles

Mount board (optional)

Spray adhesive

Vintage (or vintage-inspired) fabric

Strong glue

Drawing pins

Vintage buttons

HALF A DAY

MEDIUM

1. Carefully remove any glass from your frame and set aside. Sand the wooden edges of the frame. Brush or spray on two or three coats of paint.

2. Cover the frame backing with adhesive cork, or glue on cork tiles. If your frame doesn't have a back, cut a piece of mount board to fit, and cover this with cork instead.

3. Cut a piece of fabric to cover the cork backing, allowing an extra 5cm (2in) around all sides. Spray adhesive over the cork surface and place your fabric on top. Smooth out any wrinkles and fold the excess over the sides and stick to the back of the board.

4. Spread glue around the recess inside the edges of the frame. Press the fabric-covered board firmly into place behind the frame, and set aside to dry.

5. Glue vintage buttons to the top of your drawing pins to decorate.

CROCHETED HOT-WATER BOTTLE COVER

by Selina Steffen

A cosy multicoloured hot-water bottle cover, this crocheted
lovely can be made using any combination of colours.

YOU WILL NEED:

Yarn 100g (3½oz) ball
each of red, yellow, brown,
orange, blue and green

4mm (US size G6) crochet hook

1 DAY

MEDIUM

Please note: this project uses UK crochet terms.

1. Please note: at the end of every row, make 2 chain stitches and turn. Make 72 chain stitches, joining together to form a loop. Crochet 4 rows in dc. Change to red and work 2 more rows of dc. Change to yellow. Work 2dc into one stitch, miss a stitch and work 2dc into the next stitch. Repeat for another row.

2. Change to brown. Work 1tr, 1ch, and then 1tr into every other stitch. Work 3 rows of dc (with 70 stitches per row). Change to orange. Work 2 dc into one stitch, miss a stitch and work 2dc into the next stitch. Change to yellow and repeat for another row.

3. Change to blue. Work 1tr, followed by 1ch, followed by 1tr into every other stitch. Work a row of 2dc into every other stitch. Change to yellow. Work a row of 2dc into every other stitch. Repeat for another row. Change to brown. Work 1tr, followed by 1ch, followed by another tr into every other stitch for one row. Work 3 rows of dc.

4. Place hot-water bottle inside the crochet. Change to green. Work a row of 2dc into every other stitch. Repeat this, using a new colour for each row, in red, green, yellow and then green order. At the beginning and end of each row, reduce by one stitch. You should have 48 stitches at this stage. Change to blue. Work 1dc into every other stitch. Change to yellow and work a row of dc into each stitch. Reduce by 2 stitches at the beginning and end of both rows. Change to blue. Work a row of dc. You should have 32 stitches.

5. Work 12dc at the centre back of the hot-water bottle and repeat for 6 rows. Change to red. Work 7 rows of dc, increasing by 1 stitch at the beginning and end of each row. Work 6dc along either side of the blue section, making 3 rows of dc and join them to the edges of the red section, to form a hood.

VINTAGE PINCUSHION

by Amanda Stinton

A beautiful and practical pincushion made in floral fabric
with contrasting trims to give a vintage feel.

YOU WILL NEED:

Floral fabric 32 x 18cm (12½ x 7in)

Vintage-style ribbon 9cm (3½in)

Contrasting ric rac 18cm (7in)

Three tiny buttons

Toy stuffing

1 HOUR

MEDIUM

1. Cut two fabric rectangles each 16 x 9cm (6¼ x 3½in).

2. Take one rectangle and hand or machine sew a strip of ribbon across the width, about 5cm (2in) from the end. On the other end sew two strips of ric rac about 5cm (2in) from the end, leaving a gap of about 2cm (¾in) between each strip.

3. In between the two strips of ric rac sew on three small buttons, equally spaced as shown in the picture.

4. Pin your decorated front panel and back panel right sides together. Sew around the edges about 1.5cm (⅝in) from the edge, until you reach about 4cm (1½in) from where you started.

5. Turn the project the correct way out by gently pulling the fabric through the unsewn gap. Push the corners out to create a neat rectangle. Push stuffing through the gap until the pincushion is firmly padded. Hand sew the gap closed.

CROCHETED RAG RUG

by Shenna Swan

This gorgeous, yet practical rag rug is worked in yarn made
from old rags, using simple crochet techniques.

YOU WILL NEED:

Old T-shirts and sweatshirts
(see step 1)

10mm (US size N/P) crochet hook

2 DAYS

EASY

1. Collect old T-shirts, sweatshirts or
jumpers. Think about the colours and
textures that you want to incorporate.
Launder the garments, but don't worry
if there are stains that won't come out,
or small amounts of damage, as these
won't be visible in the finished rug.

2. Deconstruct the garments
by cutting up the side seams and
underarm seams from the welt to
the cuff. Lay each garment flat
and cut it up in a continuous strip
following around the outer edge
to create the rag yarn. The yarn
should be about 1.5cm (⅝in) wide.

3. When the garment is used up,
wind the rag yarn into balls ready to
be used. It's a good idea to prepare

plenty of rag yarn before beginning
to make the rug so you have lots of
colours and textures to choose from.

4. Using a large crochet hook make
a slip stitch and chain on about 30–40
stitches, or the width required for the
rug. Using double crochet work in
rows until the required size is reached.

5. Change the colour and texture
as required to achieve the desired
effect, or alternatively when each
ball ends, by hand stitching the
end of one ball to the beginning of
another with a few anchoring stitches.
These don't have to be neat, as they
won't show in the finished piece.

CLARICE CLIFF TEA COSY

by Linda Clements

A bright tea cosy to start your day with a smile – inspired by the colourful and cheerful crocus design made popular by Clarice Cliff in the 1920s.

YOU WILL NEED:

Cream background fabric, two pieces 21.6 x 31.8cm (8½ x 12½in)

Lining fabric, two pieces 21.6 x 31.8cm (8½ x 12½in)

Yellow sun ray appliqué fabric, 22.9 x 28cm (9 x 11in)

Green grass appliqué fabric, 7.6cm x 33cm (3 x 13in)

Fabrics for crocus appliqué: one 12.7cm (5in) square each of dark orange, medium orange, yellow and mauve

71cm (28in) of green bias binding

Fusible web

Wadding (batting), two pieces 21.6 x 31.8cm (8½ x 12½in)

Stranded cotton (floss) to match crocus appliqués and green for leaves

1DAY

HARD

1. Make the sun ray shapes following the template instructions. Pin the triangles right side up on one of the background pieces, aligning the triangle raw edges with the top of the background (the triangle points will extend past the base). Machine sew in place along the seamed edges. Make the grass shape following the template instructions and set aside.

2. Back the crocus fabrics with fusible web and prepare the appliqués following the template instructions. Fuse the appliqués to the background. Using two strands of stranded cotton and blanket stitch, edge all flowers. Machine sew the grass appliqué in position.

3. Pin wadding to the back of the patchwork and stem stitch the leaves with two strands of green embroidery thread, either freehand or using the template. Add a lining piece to the back and machine quilt if desired. Sandwich the other wadding piece between the remaining background piece and a lining piece and quilt as desired. Press all work.

4. Use the tea cosy template to cut the front and back of the cosy to shape. With right sides together, sew around the curve, turn through to the right side and press. Bind the bottom opening of the cosy.

Full-size templates for this project are available at: www.stitchcraftcreate.co.uk/patterns

HOME & GARDEN

HANDKERCHIEF HANGING VASES

by Fiona Pearce

These pretty hanging vases are made from upcycled
glass jars and dainty vintage hankerchiefs.

YOU WILL NEED:

Clean, dry glass jars
Vintage handkerchiefs or fabric
Ribbon or lace
Craft (or baling) wire
Rubber bands
Wire cutters or sharp scissors

30 MINUTES

EASY

1. To make one hanging vase, iron a
handkerchief flat, pattern side down.
Fold the bottom of the handkerchief
towards the centre and the top of
the handkerchief down to create a
band of fabric that is the same height
as the jar you wish to cover. Iron
the fabric strip to hold its shape.

2. Using wire cutters or sharp
scissors cut a 75cm (29½in) length
of craft (or baling) wire for each jar.

Wrap it tightly around the grooves in
the top of the jar, then make a wire
handle loop. Trim off any excess wire.

3. Wrap the folded handkerchief
around the vase, pattern side
showing, and secure it in place
with a rubber band. Cut a length of
ribbon or lace and tie a bow around
the vase to hide the rubber band.

4. Fill the jar with water and flowers.

CLIPPY FELT CUSHION

by Julia Liddell

This cosy felt cushion has a central heart design,
made using the clever clippy mat technique.

YOU WILL NEED:

Two pieces felt, 40 x
40cm (15¾ x 15¾in)

One piece felt, 60 x
30cm (23½ x 12in)

One piece hessian, 25 x
25cm (10 x 10in)

Large embroidery hoop
30cm (12in) diameter

Cushion filler

Embroidery threads and
beads (optional)

1. Cut the 60 x 30cm (23½ x 12in)
piece of felt into strips measuring 10
x 2cm (4 x ¾in). Take one of the 40 x
40cm (15¾ x 15¾in) felt pieces and
cut a heart shape in the centre. Place
a piece of hessian behind and stitch
in place around the heart. Place in
the hoop and centralize the heart.

2. Working from behind and in
rows, poke a piece of off-cut felt
through the hessian. Poke the other
end about three strings away. Poke
another piece through the same hole
you have just used. Continue the
lines until all the hessian is covered,
with the fluffy heart on the right
side, and no hessian is visible.

3. Remove from the frame and
gently press the reverse to remove any
marks. Using the other piece of felt,
place the right sides together. Stitch
around the outside, leaving a gap of
12cm (4¾in) in the centre of one
seam. Snip the corners to remove any
excess. Turn through to right side.

4. Stuff the cushion with filler
through the hole, ensuring corners
are filled. Using a strong thread,
close the hole with small stitches
to ensure filler does not 'leak'.

5. You can further embellish
the cushion using embroidery
threads, beads and such like.

2 HOURS

MEDIUM

VINTAGE CASE

by Sarah Oatley

A vintage-inspired sewing case just like the ones that mothers and grandmothers had for storing their sewing bits and bobs. This useful wallet uses vintage lace and ribbons for holding threads.

YOU WILL NEED:

Vintage fabric – amount depends on desired size of case

Vintage lace

Elastic

Ribbon

Decorations and buttons

Stiff interfacing

1. Cut two pieces of fabric one and a half times the length of the desired case. Sew the fabric, right sides together, along the two long sides and one short side. Turn the piece right side out.

2. Cut interfacing to fit the entire length of the case and insert between the sewn fabrics. Sew the final short side closed.

3. Fold over the ends to create a pocket on either end of the long side. The pockets should be a quarter of the size of the long side. Sew the sides to secure the pockets.

4. Add ribbons and elastic to make straps to hold sewing items. Sew a length of ribbon or lace onto the top edge of one end as a closure for the case. It should be twice the length of a short side.

5. Decorate the outside with further lace, ribbons or buttons as desired.

1 HOUR

MEDIUM

SOYA CANDLES IN VINTAGE GLASS

by Jacky Massos

Collect pretty old-fashioned glass jars and drinking glasses, or perhaps bone china, then pour scented soya wax into these lovely vintage containers.

YOU WILL NEED:

Vintage glass or china container

Soya wax

Essential oils

Wick with metal base

Large saucepan with smaller pan to create a double boiler

Glue gun

30 MINUTES

EASY

1. To prepare the container make sure that it is very clean and dry. Stick your metal base wick with a little glue to the centre of the base of the glass or china. I use a little melted wax over a teaspoon to keep the wick in place.

2. Measure how much liquid your container holds, then weigh out that amount of soya wax less 10%. Heat the water to simmering. Add the pan of soya wax and melt on a low heat, stirring a little.

3. To add your essential oils to the melted wax, stir in a few drops (no more than 5% of your volume of wax) and stir gently to distribute.

4. Pour into your prepared glass or china container. Leave to cool for 24 hours before using, and then snip the wick to 5mm (¼in).

Please note: do not leave lit candles unattended. You can re-use your container as soya wax is water based with a low burning temperature.

FAIR ISLE HOT-WATER BOTTLE COVER

by Ellen Kharade

A snuggly hot water bottle cover is made from up-cycling
an old vintage Fair-Isle-style sweater.

YOU WILL NEED:

Fair-Isle-style woollen sweater

Vintage style buttons

Decorative braid or ribbon

Large darning needle

Sewing machine

2 HOURS

EASY

1. Cut the sweater up into a back and front. Lay the three templates over the fabric placing them well over the patterned areas. Cut out the two back pieces and front piece of the cover.

2. Hem the raw edges of the top and bottom back pieces. Using a sewing machine or by hand make three buttonholes across the top of the back piece. Sew vintage-style buttons in corresponding places across the bottom half of the back cover.

3. With the right sides facing, lay the top and bottom back pieces over the front, matching up the seams as you do so. Pin and machine stitch into place.

4. At the neck of the hot-water bottle thread through a decorative ribbon using a large darning needle.

5. Sew on a few vintage buttons at the neck to finish. You could make a yo-yo as an additional decoration.

Full-size templates for this project are available at: www.stitchcraftcreate.co.uk/patterns

HOME & GARDEN

POSH PEG BAG

by Lisa Fordham

This clothes peg bag is made of hard-wearing laminated cloth to keep it smart for ages. It's a great way to brighten up your laundry day.

YOU WILL NEED:

Laminated fabric 0.25m (¼yd) x 54–56cm (21¼–22in) wide

Bias binding 60cm (24in) x 2.5cm (1in) wide, cut in two equal pieces

One wire coat hanger

Plastic tape (optional)

2 HOURS

EASY

1. Using the template draw one back and two front pieces on the laminated fabric, allowing an extra 1cm (⅜in) seam allowance all around. Line up the coat hanger and bend to fit the top of the bag. Set the hanger aside.

2. Carefully cut out one back piece of laminated fabric and two front pieces ensuring that you have enough fabric to overlap at the opening. Lay out your two front pieces right side up and cut two lengths of bias binding to fit along the top of the bottom piece, and the bottom of the

top piece (that is, the bag opening). With right sides together, fold the bias binding lengthways over the top of the bottom front and pin into position. Repeat on the bottom of the top piece. Machine stitch into place using a 1cm (⅜in) seam allowance.

3. With right sides together, pin the back, bottom front and top front together, ensuring there is a 1cm (⅜in) overlap at the opening. The bias binding on the bottom front should sit neatly behind the bias binding at the top.

4. Mark the area where the coat hanger comes through the top of the bag using a pin each side of the 3cm (1¼in) space (that is, the space for the hanger). Pin, tack and then starting at the top of the bag carefully machine stitch all around using a 1cm (⅜in) seam. When complete turn the bag right side out and slip in the hanger.

5. Wrap plastic tape around the hook to finish, if required.

Full-size templates for this project are available at: www.stitchcraftcreate.co.uk/patterns

HOME & GARDEN

TIN FLOWER CENTREPIECE

by Elsie Molyneux of Elsie Mo Flowers

This easy project is a great way to recycle old tins, jars and crockery to bring the outdoors in. Use any variety of fresh flowers that are in season.

YOU WILL NEED:

One block of floral foam

Container

Moss

Variety of fresh flowers

Grasses or foliage (e.g. bear grass)

30 MINUTES

EASY

1. Choose a container you like that is no longer used but too good to throw away, for example vintage tins (or modern food tins if you soak off the labels) or old crockery (bowls or teacups). Jam jars can also be used if you paint the inside.

2. Cut your floral foam to the right size and soak by floating it in a bowl full of water. It will absorb and sink when it's ready (don't force it under). Fill your chosen container to the lip with floral foam so it reaches all the edges.

3. Choose a natural looking selection of flowers from your garden or florist shop (so you can buy stems individually). Don't over complicate the look of the design, but choose a maximum of four different flower types as different from each other as possible. Smaller flower heads are easier to work with, and picking a colour scheme also helps.

4. Insert your flowers and foliage into the floral foam in an upright manner to resemble natural growing formations. Disperse them randomly

to cover the whole surface of the foam. Add grasses and a touch of foliage to add to the garden theme.

5. Finally, fill in the gaps between the flowers with moss evenly to create a lawn like effect. Moss can be bought in garden centres or you may be lucky enough to find it in your garden. Alternatively, small stones, pebbles or decorative gravel could be used.

VINTAGE JELLY MOULD CANDLES

by *Kirsty Neale*

Small, vintage jelly moulds made of metal or glass, are filled with a
wick and melted wax to make these simple but striking candles.

YOU WILL NEED:

Small vintage jelly mould

Candle wick

Metal wick-holder

Pencil

Candle wax

Saucepan

Heatproof bowl to fit inside saucepan

Essential oil (optional)

Cocktail stick

2 HOURS

EASY

1. Cut a length of wick, 5cm (2in) taller than the height of the mould. Thread one end through a metal wick-holder and place in the bottom of the mould. Tie the other end around a pencil. Rest this across the top of the mould to hold the wick in position.

2. Place your wax in a heatproof bowl and place the bowl over a saucepan half-filled with water. Gently heat the water until the wax in the bowl is completely melted. Stir in a few drops of essential oil if you want to make a scented candle.

3. Carefully pour the liquid wax into the mould, and allow to cool for 30–60 minutes.

4. As the wax hardens, a well or dip is likely to form in the centre. To even out the surface, melt a small amount of wax and use a cocktail stick to make holes around the wick. Pour the melted wax carefully on top.

5. Trim the wick so only 1cm (⅜in) or so is visible above the top of the wax. Set your finished candle aside for 24 hours before lighting.

CLOAK HANGER

by Claire Garland

Tweedy-look cloak hangers with an air of elegance – experiment with colour combinations and embellish with pom poms for that truly retro look.

YOU WILL NEED:

1 x 50g (1¾oz) ball any Aran or worsted weight yarn in green – MC

1 x 50g (1¾oz) ball any Aran or worsted weight yarn in light pink – CC

Pom pom maker

4.5mm (US size 7) knitting needles

Tension: 19 sts x 28 rows = 10cm in stocking stitch

3 HOURS

MEDIUM

1. In MC, cast on 22sts.

Row 1: (WS) K.
Row 2: (RS) Using CC [k1, sl1 p-wise with yarn at back] 11 times.
Row 3: Using CC [sl1 p-wise with yarn at back, k1] 11 times.
Row 4: Using MC [sl1 p-wise with yarn at back, p1] 11 times.
Row 5: Using MC [p1, sl1 p-wise with yarn at back] 11 times.
Rep last 4 rows until the length of the knitted fabric matches the length of your coat hanger, ending with a WS row – finish with a p row before casting off k-wise.

2. Fold the cover over your hanger with the cast on/cast off edges against the short ends and the row ends at the lower edge – the hook slips through a knitted stitch. Over sew around all three sides.

3. Make two pom poms using the medium-sized disks, both shades of yarn at once and following the manufacturer's instructions.

4. Embellish with the pom poms or embellish with silk flowers, fabric ribbon or vintage buttons.

GOLD LEAF AND RIBBON VASE

by Lucy Morris

This is a simple idea for decorating vases or jars for special
occasions using gold leaf paint and grosgrain ribbon.

YOU WILL NEED:

Small glass jar or vase

Classic Liquid Leaf Metallic
Gold paint (available online)

Flat paintbrush or small
sponge paint applicator

Glue gun or craft glue

Masking tape

Grosgrain ribbon

30 MINUTES

MEDIUM

1. Choose your glass vase or jar.
This works best on a small item
such as a jam jar or small milk
bottle. These can be collected from
antique fairs and junk shops easily
and cheaply. Ensure that the glass
is clean and dry before you begin.

2. Run masking tape around the
bottle halfway up the side to create a
clean line. Shake the metallic paint
well and apply smoothly with broad
strokes to the lower half of the bottle
ensuring that the paint doesn't go
above the top line of the masking tape.

3. When you have a smooth
coat, allow it to dry for 20 minutes,
then carefully remove the masking
tape. Heat your glue gun or apply
craft glue around the top line of
the gold paint and secure grosgrain
ribbon carefully. Allow to dry.

4. Fill with pretty country
flowers and arrange in clusters of
varying heights for a charming
vintage-style flower display.

1950s-INSPIRED PINNY

by Philippa Belcher-Love

Make this cute little pinafore, so you can look
glamorous even when doing the housework!

YOU WILL NEED:

Pencil and paper

Wide fabric ribbon 140cm (55in)

Fabric 0.5m (½yd)

Ric rac (for edge) 120cm (48in)

Ric rac (for pocket tops) 60cm (12in)

Lace trim 180cm (71in)

Sewing machine

1. Enlarge and cut out the
template. Cut out one apron,
on the fold, and two pockets.

2. Mark the pocket locations and
sew in the pleats, as indicated.

3. Turn the apron edges under by
5mm (¼in), twice, so no raw edges are
showing. Do the same to the pockets
and turn under the top edge, from the
line as marked on the template. Place
the pockets on the apron as marked on
the template, and sew into position.

4. Gather the lace trim and tack to
the edge of the apron. Tack ric rac
around the edge of the apron. Sew
through all layers with a neat stich,
by either machine or hand. Cut the
remaining piece of ric rac in half and
hand sew each piece to the pocket tops.

5. Match the centre of the ribbon
to the centre of the apron on the right
side, and sew on. Cut ribbon ends at
an angle to stop fraying, or stich a hem.

2 HOURS

EASY

Full-size templates for this project are available at: www.stitchcraftcreate.co.uk/patterns

HOME & GARDEN

ELEGANT BUREAU TIDY

by Danielle Lowy

Bring some floral elegance to the office with a desk tidy that cleverly uses scraps left over from other vintage craft projects.

YOU WILL NEED:

Tin can
Material scraps
Clear-drying glue
Lace or ribbons
Pinking shears

1. With the pinking shears, cut about 16 strips each 13 x 2cm (5 x ¾in) from your material scraps. File down any sharp edges on your tin can.

2. Glue the strips onto the tin in overlapping lines and fold the excess material within the tin, glueing it down.

3. Cut out a medium-sized heart with pinking shears and glue it on the middle of the tin. Cut and glue a smaller heart on top.

4. Decorate the tin as you like, glueing ribbon or lace trims around the top and bottom of the tin.

1 HOUR

EASY

PRETTY TEACUP CANDLE

by Maggie Jones

This simple project uses re-melted candle wax and a vintage teacup to make a pretty, upcycled candle.

YOU WILL NEED:

Suitable cups

Old wax candles

Candle wick in thin or medium

Thin wire

Glue dots

Old saucepan

Old heat-resistant bowl to fit inside saucepan

Plastic jug

1. Only use old candles that are clean with no scorch marks on them. To melt the wax use a saucepan and a suitable bowl (for example, Pyrex). Don't use this equipment for food preparation. Fill the saucepan a quarter to a third full with water. Sit the bowl inside. Heat the water until it is boiling. Place the wax into the bowl, keeping the water simmering, and ensuring it doesn't bubble into the bowl.

2. Prepare your teacup. Note that the smaller the cup, the thinner the wick you need to use. Cut the wick 3cm (1¼in) longer than final length and dip in molten wax to stiffen it. When

dry, fix to the bottom of teacup using a glue dot. To ensure the wick stays upright, thread wire through the end of the wick supporting this on the cup.

3. When melted, remove old wicks and transfer the wax into a plastic jug and pour into the teacup, being careful not to disturb the wick. Fill to about 2cm (¾in) from the top. Put un-used wax back into the bowl and keep warm.

4. As the wax in the cup hardens you will see a well forming. Re-melt the wax in the bowl and top up the wax in the cup. When the wax hardens, take out the wire and trim the wick.

Never leave a burning candle unattended. Don't put melted wax down the sink, as it will block pipes. Let it set, skim it off and put in the bin. When using old candles, keep colours similar. Mixing too many colours will result in a murky brown shade.

1 HOUR

EASY

VINTAGE DOILY COASTERS

by Kirsty Neale

These tea-party coasters are made by pressing a vintage doily onto circles of white modelling clay for added texture and prettiness.

YOU WILL NEED:

White air-drying clay

Rolling pin

Vintage doily

Large cookie cutter or round metal container

Clear varnish

Thick coloured felt

1. Break off a piece of clay and soften it by rolling between your palms. Place on a flat surface and roll out to a thickness of about 1cm (⅜in).

2. Place a vintage doily on top, so it covers around half of the clay. Press it down gently, first with your fingers and then with a rolling pin. Carefully peel the doily off and set it aside.

3. Using a large cookie cutter or the rim of a round metal container, cut out a circle from the clay. Position your cutter so you include some plain clay and some with the doily impression. Leave the clay to dry, according to the instructions on the packaging.

4. To seal the clay, as well as give it a glossy, porcelain-like finish, brush or spray on two or three coats of clear varnish. Make sure you allow each layer to dry before adding the next.

5. Finally, cut out a piece of felt the same size as the finished coaster. Glue it to the base of the clay, to protect your table from scratches and add a subtle splash of colour to your tea party.

1 DAY

EASY

ANTIQUE DOILY CUSHION

by Linda Clements

This pretty cushion is ideal for using up odd squares of fabrics, or displaying some antique lace doilies. If you like to crochet then you could make your own doilies.

YOU WILL NEED:

Mixed pastel prints, a total of eighteen 9cm (3½in) squares

Two strips white print each 4.4 x 47cm (1¾ x 18½in)

Top and bottom border: two strips pastel print, each 4.4 x 47cm (1¾ x 18½in)

Left border: one strip pastel print, 4.4 x 36.8cm (1¾ x 14½in)

Right border and lining: one strip pastel print 15.2 x 72.4cm (6in x 28½in)

Backing fabric, 53.3 x 50.2cm (19¾ x 14½in)

Wadding (batting) 48.3 x 35.5cm (19 x 14in)

Two lace doilies

Eight medium buttons

Cushion pad

HALF A DAY

MEDIUM

1. Make the patchwork by joining six squares together into three rows using 6mm (¼in) seams. Press seams in one direction. Sew a white strip between each row of squares and press. Sew on the top and bottom border strips, then the left-hand strip and press. Don't sew the right border yet.

2. Sew the backing fabric to the bottom of the cushion (along the long edge). Now sew the final border to the right side of the combined patchwork/backing piece. Hem the raw edge of this strip.

3. Sew the doilies to the cushion using matching thread. Add the wadding to the back of the patchwork and machine quilt around the doilies in two circles of zigzag stitch.

4. Fold the patchwork and backing right sides together and sew along the top edge. Turn through and press. Turn the right-hand border in by half its width, press and insert the cushion pad.

5. Position four buttons equally spaced along the right side, with four matching at the back. Sew through each pair of buttons to fasten the cushion.

VINTAGE SEWER'S HELPER

by Fiona-Grace Peppler

A pretty teacup and some old-fashioned tricks can keep your pins
and needles clean and sharp, ready for all your sewing projects.

YOU WILL NEED:

Vintage teacup and saucer

Vintage teaspoon

Coordinating cotton

Bird grit (from pet shops)

Fine wire wool

Strong magnets

Superglue or ceramic cement

Tailor's chalk

1. Glue the magnets to the inside of the teacup, low down, but not on the base. These will capture pins, needles and scissors placed in the saucer for safekeeping. Glue the teacup into the saucer and set aside to dry.

2. Make the pincushion by cutting a circle of cotton about three times larger than the top of the cup. Hand sew a ring of running stitch about 5mm (¼in) in from the raw edge, but don't fasten off.

3. Pull on your sewing thread to gather the circle. Stuff the ball with bird grit. This will keep your pins rust free and sharpen them when you use it. Close the puff and fasten off tightly.

4. Create a smaller cushion in the same way to fit the bowl of your teaspoon, but this time stuff it with fine wire wool. This is your needle sharpener – but don't store your needles here, as they will rust. Carefully glue the pad into the spoon.

5. Now assemble the final pieces by positioning the pincushion into the cup and carefully gluing into place.

2 HOURS
EASY

'SPOT OF TEA?' COSY

by Claire Garland

This knitted, retro-style tea cosy is as cheery as a bunch of red cherries
and will brighten up any teatime treat. It fits any six-cup teapot.

YOU WILL NEED:

1 x 50g (1¾oz) ball any Aran or
worsted weight yarn in red – MC

1 x 50g (1¾oz) ball any Aran or
worsted weight yarn in cream – CC

Pom pom maker

4.5mm (US size 7) knitting needles

*Tension: 20sts x 25 rows =
10cm in stocking stitch*

3 HOURS

EASY

1. Sides (make 2)

In MC cast on 38sts.

Row 1: *K2, p1, rep from *
across to last 2 sts, k2.
Row 2: *P2, k1, rep from *
across to last 2 sts, p2.
Rep last 2 rows once.
Row 5: (RS) Using CC, k6, [turn,
p4, turn, sl1, k3, sl1, k5] 5 times,
turn, p4, turn, sl1, k3, sl1, k1.
Row 6: (WS) Using CC p1, sl1,
[p5, turn, k4, turn, sl1, p3, sl1] 5
times, p5, turn, k4, turn, sl1, p4.
Row 7: Using MC k.
Row 8: Using MC p.
Row 9: (RS) Using CC k3, turn,
p2, turn, sl1, k1, sl1, k5, [turn,

p4, turn, sl1, k3, sl1, k5] 4
times, turn, p4, turn, sl 1, k3,
k4, turn, p3, turn, sl1, k2.
Row 10: (WS) Using CC p4, turn,
k3, turn, sl1, p2, sl1, [p5, turn,
k4, turn, sl1, p3, sl1] 5 times,
p3, turn, k2, turn, sl1, p1.
Row 11: as Row 7.
Row 12: as Row 8.
Rep last 8 rows twice.
Cut yarn CC.
Row 29: (RS) (dec) Using MC k1,
[k2 tog] 18 times, k1. 20sts
Row 30: *P2, k1, rep from *
across to last 2sts, k2.
Row 31: *K2, p1, rep from *
across to last 2sts, k2.

2. Eyelets

Row 32: *P1, yo, k2 tog, rep from
* across to last 2sts, p1, yo, k1.
Row 33: *K2, p1, rep from * across.
Row 34: *K1, p2, rep from * across.
Rep last 2 rows three times.
Cast off in rib as set.

3.
Join the two side seams leaving
spaces for the teapot handle and spout.

4.
Cut two 40cm (15¾in) lengths
in contrasting strands of yarn and
thread through the eyelets. Make two
medium-sized pom poms, with both
shades of yarn at once. Sew the pom
poms onto the ends of the lengths.

SHABBY CHIC SHED ADORNMENT

by Danielle Lowy

Show the garden shed some love with this gorgeous shabby chic
heart – perfect for using up broken jewellery and random buttons.

YOU WILL NEED:

Garden wire, 1–2mm
($\frac{1}{32}$–$\frac{1}{16}$in) thick

Pliers or strong scissors

50 assorted buttons, beads and
broken jewellery, with holes big
enough for the wire to fit through

Ribbon 50cm (20in)

1 HOUR

EASY

1. Place your buttons,
beads and broken jewellery
items in a heart shape.

2. Cut 50cm (20in) of garden
wire and bend it in half.

3. Thread beads and buttons up
one half of the heart shape from
the bent middle. Thread the other
side so they are filled to the same
length. Don't worry if it doesn't
look like a heart shape yet.

4. Twist the two wires together
at the back to secure them. Make
a hanging loop from one piece
of wire. Cut off any excess.

5. Tie the ribbon to the bottom of
the loop, wrap it around the hanging
loop and finish with a bow. Now
ease the wire into a heart shape.

CHAIR-BACK TIDY

by Penny Fitzmaurice

An easy-to-make tidy with a pocket for papers that can be made from
a favourite vintage fabric and slipped over the back of a chair.

YOU WILL NEED:

Vintage fabric, about 28 x 45cm
(11 x 18in), plus enough for motif

Plain cotton or linen fabric,
about 60 x 45cm (24 x 18in)

Sewing machine (optional)

2 HOURS

EASY

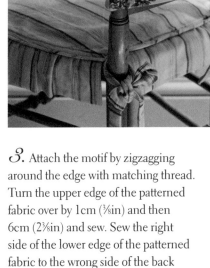

1. Measure width of chair back at
widest point. Cut one piece of plain
fabric 60cm (24in) x width of chair
plus 3cm (1¼in). Cut one piece of
vintage patterned fabric 28cm (11in)
x width of chair plus 3cm (1¼in).

2. Cut generously around a motif
in your vintage fabric or cut a simple
shape of your own design. Press all
pieces. Fold the large piece in half
across the width and press to mark
the top. Open out, position the motif
centrally on one side and pin. This
is the front. Turn the edge over by
5mm (¼in), twice, and then sew.

3. Attach the motif by zigzagging
around the edge with matching thread.
Turn the upper edge of the patterned
fabric over by 1cm (⅜in) and then
6cm (2⅜in) and sew. Sew the right
side of the lower edge of the patterned
fabric to the wrong side of the back
lower edge, using a 1.5cm (⅝in) seam.
Zigzag to neaten and then press.

4. Press the pocket up, right side
facing. Fold the front down over the
pocket, right sides together, aligning
lower edges. Pin the sides. Check the
fit on the chair. Sew side seams, zigzag
edges to neaten. Turn and press.

GILDED VINTAGE FRAME

by Ellen Kharade

A junk-shop vintage picture frame is given a new lease of life by gilding with 9ct gold leaf. For a real vintage look, you could use it to display an antique sepia photograph.

YOU WILL NEED:

Old junk-shop picture frame

Acrylic primer paint

Paintbrush

Bristle brushes

Gold-leaf size

9ct gold leaf, loose

Soft, clean cloth

2 HOURS

MEDIUM

1. Using a wide, bristle brush, apply a thin undercoat of acrylic primer paint to the frame and leave for several hours to dry out. Using a wide dust-free bristle brush, apply a coating of gold-leaf size to the frame, making sure that it is completely covered. Leave the frame in a dust-free environment for at least 12 to 24 hours for the size to become tacky.

2. Carefully pick up the gold leaf using the corner of a paintbrush and gently lay it over the frame. Press the leaf onto the frame using the brush.

3. Continue in this way until the frame is completely covered, taking care not to miss out any areas. Stray bits of gold leaf can be picked up and re-applied to sized areas.

4. Once completed, gently brush with a large bristle brush to remove any stray bits of gold leaf.

5. Using a soft cloth or a large piece of cotton wool gently rub over the frame to burnish the leaf to a soft sheen and to make sure the gold has adhered well to the frame.

RETRO PHONE BOX MOBILE CASE

by Kirsty Neale

A very British icon, a traditional red phone box, makes a quirky cover for your mobile (cell) phone. Fusible web appliqué makes this a really quick project.

YOU WILL NEED:

Red felt

Fusible web

Vintage-style patterned fabric

Black thread

Inkjet-friendly fabric

Access to a computer and printer

Ribbon

Sewing machine

2 DAYS

MEDIUM

1. Copy the phone box template onto felt and cut out twice. Draw an 8.5 x 6.5cm (3¼ x 2½in) rectangle onto fusible web, iron onto the back of your patterned fabric and cut out. Peel away the backing paper and iron the rectangle onto one of the felt phone box pieces.

2. Machine stitch around the edges of the patterned rectangle, using black thread. Add two extra vertical lines of stitching and two horizontally to create a window pane effect. Stitch over all lines a second time to create an optional sketchy look.

3. Print the word 'telephone' onto an inkjet-friendly fabric sheet, using a simple, elegant font. It should measure roughly 6 x 1cm (2⅜ x ⅜in). Cut out, leaving a narrow border around the word. Stitch into place on the felt phone box, just above the patterned fabric rectangle.

4. Again using black thread, stitch twice around the top part of the felt phone box, as marked on the template. Cut a 3.5cm (1⅜in) piece of ribbon and fold it in half. Pin to one side of the felt phone box piece, just below the stitched section.

5. Pin the decorated felt piece to the plain one, so the ribbon ends are sandwiched in between. Sew along the side and bottom edges to join the two pieces together, using a double line of stitches, as before.

Full-size templates for this project are available at: www.stitchcraftcreate.co.uk/patterns

HOME & GARDEN

SUFFOLK PUFFS IDEAS

by Daisy Bryan

Here's how to make Suffolk puffs, which are also called yo-yos, and use them to great effect around your home, on cushion covers and lampshades, as well as on jewellery.

YOU WILL NEED:

Circular object to draw around (see step 1)

Pen

Piece of fabric

Strong thread

Needle

15 MINUTES

EASY

1. The fabric circle size needs to be twice the diameter of the finished yo-yo, plus 1.3cm (½in) for a hem. Start by drawing around your circular object onto the back of your fabric and then cut out the circle.

2. Tie a knot in the end of a long piece of thread and sew a running stitch along the edge of the circle. To be really neat, fold the edge over as you go to form a basic hem.

3. When you have stitched all the way around the circle hold the fabric and pull the thread through from both ends (find your original knot) to gather it.

4. Pull tight and tie the two ends together, then trim away any excess thread. And there you have a Suffolk puff! Make lots more puffs in the same way.

5. Now you can use your puffs to decorate anything you like – cushions, lampshades, clothes, and so on.

This technique dates back to the Victorian era, when puffs made from scraps of fabric were sewn together to make patchwork quilts.

CHICKEN EGG COSY

by Claire Garland

Get cracking on this cheerful knitted and crocheted chicken.
She's full of vintage style and is sure to make breakfast a fun time.

YOU WILL NEED:

1 x 50g (1¾oz) ball cream
DK yarn – MC

Small amount of orange
coloured yarn – CC

Half a 50g (1¾oz) ball
of blue yarn – CC1

Set 3.5mm (US size 4) double
pointed needles (dpns)

3.00mm (US size C) crochet hook

Two small mis-matched
vintage buttons

Tapestry needle size 22

*Tension: 24sts x 29 rows =
10cm in stocking stitch*

2 HOURS

MEDIUM

Please note: this project uses UK crochet terms.

1. Chicken

In CC cast on 16sts and then use simple sock toe to complete the cast on as follows:

A. Hold needle with stitches in left hand.

B. Hold two empty dpns parallel in right hand.

C. Slip 1st cast on st p-wise onto the dpn closest to you and off the needle in the left hand, then slip the next cast on st onto the dpn furthest away and off the RH needle.

Repeat step C until all 16 stitches are divided onto the two parallel dpns, 8 sts on the front dpn and 8 sts on the back. Slide sts to the other ends of the dpns, working yarn at back.

RS facing, cont working in the rnd, beginning by knitting the sts on the back dpn – work stitches over two dpns, using a 3rd dpn to knit with:

Rnd1: K16.
Rnd 2: K16, turn and work so that you are no longer working in the round and with WS of work facing.
Row 3: K15.
Row 4: K14.
Row 5: K13.
Row 6: K14. Join into the round – therefore do not turn the work and cont as follows.

Rnd 7: K16. Cut yarn CC.
Rnd 8: Using MC k16.
Rnd 9: (inc) K1, kf&b, k4, kf&b, k1, k1, kf&b, k4, kf&b, k1. 20sts
Rnds 10, 12: K.
Rnd 11: (inc) K1, kf&b, k6, kf&b, k1, k1, kf&b, k6, kf&b, k1. 24sts
Rnd 13: (inc) K10, [m1, k1] twice, [k1, m1] twice, k10. 28sts
Rnd 14: (dec) K11, cast off 6, k10. 22sts
Rnd 15: K11 then cont to knit the 11sts on the other needle under the beak.
Rnd 16: (inc) K1, kf&b, k9, k9, kf&b, k1. 24sts
Rnds 17, 19, 21, 23: K.
Rnd 18: (inc) K1, kf&b, k10, k10, kf&b, k1. 26sts
Rnd 20: (inc) K1, kf&b, k11, k11, kf&b, k1. 28sts
Rnd 22: (inc) K1, kf&b, k12, k12, kf&b, k1. 30sts
Cast off. Weave in end.
Work a couple of stitches under the beak to close the gap.

2. Ruffled feathers

With the crochet hook and yarn CC1, work 1dc into each 30 cast off stitches. Sl st into first dc to join into rnd.
Rnd 2: Insert hook through front loop of first dc then work (front loops only on this rnd) *1dc into first dc, 1htr into next dc, 5tr into next dc, 1htr into next dc, 1dc into next dc, rep from * around. Sl st in first dc. Fasten off.
Rnd 3: Work this round out of the remaining back loops of Rnd 1,

as follows: with RS facing ch3 (counts as 1tr), work 1tr into same place. Work 1tr into next st, *2tr into next st, 1tr into next st* rep from * around. Sl st in 3rd ch.
Rnd 4: *1dc into first tr, 1htr into next dc, 5tr into next dc, 1htr into next dc, 1dc into next dc, rep from * around. Sl st in first dc. Fasten off.

3. Sew buttons on for eyes to finish your chicken egg cosy – and make as many as you like.

DÉCOUPAGE MATCHBOXES

by Lotte Oldfield

Make your matchboxes pretty enough to keep on show.
These also make lovely gifts for people who have log fires.

YOU WILL NEED:

New box of matches

Découpage paper or A4- (letter-)
sized magazine picture

Brush

PVA glue

30 MINUTES

EASY

1. Remove the matchbox sleeve.
Cut up squares and strips of pretty
découpage paper or vintage-looking
magazine pictures. Keeping them to
right-angled squares and rectangles
will make covering the box easier.

2. Take the PVA glue and a brush
and start gluing longer pieces around
the sides of the box that you strike the
matches on, taking care not to go over
this striking area. Pieces can overlap
onto the top and bottom of the box.

3. When gluing, take all the pieces
right to the edges of the box but
don't overlap them into the inside
of the box as this could make the
matchbox drawer catch when in use.

4. Cover all sides (apart from
the striking strips) until the original
box doesn't show through. Put
aside and allow to dry slowly.

5. When dry replace the drawer of
matches and they are ready to use.

VINTAGE NEEDLEBOOK

by Amanda Stinton

A neat little needlebook for keeping all your pins and needles safe,
with a handy tape measure ribbon to keep it closed.

YOU WILL NEED:

Patterned fabric 18 x 11cm (7 x 4¼in)

Plain fabric 18 x 11cm (7 x 4¼in)

Two pieces tape measure
ribbon, 12cm (4¾in) long

Two pieces contrasting felt
14 x 7cm (5½ x 2¾in)

1 HOUR

EASY

1. Cut two rectangles of fabric about 18 x 11cm (7 x 4¼in). Lay the patterned piece that will be on the outside of your needlebook face up. Lay one piece of ribbon face up on top of fabric about half way down left hand edge. Repeat on right hand side. Sew in place.

2. Pin the second piece of fabric face down on top of the patterned fabric. Ensure that the ribbon is sandwiched inside both layers and isn't

showing. Sew the two pieces together, about 1.5cm (⅝in) from the edge. Leave an unsewn gap of about 4cm (1½in) when you return to where you started sewing, for turning through.

3. Carefully turn the needlebook the correct way out by gently pulling the fabric through the gap and pushing the corners out to create a neat shape. The two pieces of the ribbon will now be on the outside, creating the ties. Hand sew the gap closed.

4. For a neat finish, press your needlebook with a warm iron. Fold in half and press down the middle to create a crisp edge along the spine of the case.

5. Take your two pieces of felt and fold in half. Place on top of the inside of your needlebook so the centre folds are level. Sew down the centre line to attach both pieces of felt to needlebook. Put pins and needles into felt and tie closed using the ribbon ties.

GLAMOROUS HERB POTS

by Danielle Lowy

Make a feature of supermarket-bought herb pots by sprucing them up
with your own pot cover design, made from vintage papers.

YOU WILL NEED:

Small square plastic herb pot
(remove the herbs and soil)

Decorative vintage card,
paper or wrapping paper

Glue gun

Laminator and one A4
(letter) laminating sheet

String

Cocktail stick (or toothpick)

Hole punch

Indelible felt pen

1 HOUR

MEDIUM

1. Using one side of your herb
pot, trace round to make card
template. Use this to trace and cut
out four shapes on your chosen
decorative paper or card.

2. From the same card or
paper, cut out a heart shape.

3. Place the five shapes in the
laminating pouch, laminate
them and cut them out.

4. Glue gun three sides together on
their inside seams. With this part-made
pot lying down, insert the herb pot
and squirt a thin line of glue along
the two open seams, quickly adding
the fourth side before the glue dries.
Add the soil and herbs to the pot.

5. Write the herb name on the
heart shape. Make a hole near the
top for the string. Tie around the
stick and place it in the pot.

VINTAGE BEDROOM CUSHION

by *Penny Fitzmaurice*

Use a pretty, embroidered tray cloth to make a quick and
unique cushion to decorate your vintage boudoir.

YOU WILL NEED:

Rectangular vintage tray cloth

Square of cotton lining

Rectangle of fabric for cushion back

Coordinating bias binding,
tape or ribbon

Decorative button or bow

Three vintage buttons

Lining off-cuts

Wadding (batting)

1. Pin mark the centre of long side of tray cloth. Make it into a square by pressing in the sides to create a central, inverted box pleat. Cut a square of lining to same size. In cushion back fabric cut a rectangle 18cm (7in) wider than the square, then cut this in half.

2. On the short, central edge of each back piece, turn 1cm (⅜in) over and machine stitch. Fold over 4cm (1½in) on each to create facings and press. On one side mark three vertical buttonholes (to the size of your buttons), 2cm (¾in) in from the edge. Sew the buttonholes.

3. Working on a flat surface, overlap the facings directly one on top of the other and pin. With wrong sides together pin the square lining to the back. Check the alignment and trim if necessary to a neat square. Pin the folded tray cloth, embroidery uppermost, carefully over the top of lining (pins facing towards centre).

4. With pins, mark a line 2–3cm (¾–1⅛in) in from the edge (depending on the tray cloth design) all around the cover. Machine stitch carefully along this pin line, sewing all three layers together.

5. Fold bias binding, tape or ribbon over raw edges to bind together. Pin carefully, paying attention to corners, and then sew. Sew a button or bow to the front centre of the cushion and also buttons on the reverse. Make a pad 1.5cm (⅝in) bigger than your cover using lining off-cuts and wadding, and use this to fill your cover.

2 HOURS

EASY

MANTELPIECE SCOTTIE DOG

by Sue Trevor

A Scottie dog is as popular an image today as it was in bygone years.
This one is made from felt and wears a tartan bow.

YOU WILL NEED:

Black felt 22 x 30cm (8½ x 12in)

Small buttons for eyes

Small black beads for nose

Pre-made ribbon bow
(or make your own)

Black stranded cotton (floss)

Toy stuffing

1. Using the templates cut out two Scottie dog shapes and a base.

2. Sew these together using an embroidery thread with blanket stitch, inserting the base at the bottom. Sew along one side of the dog base to one side of the body and the same to the other.

3. Before you complete the sewing, leave a gap to stuff the dog with toy stuffing. Fill with stuffing and then finish sewing with the embroidery thread.

4. Hand sew a little black bead for its nose and two buttons for its eyes and a little bow on its neck.

5. Now make another dog, and place one on each end of your mantelpiece.

HALF A DAY

EASY

Full-size templates for this project are available at: www.stitchcraftcreate.co.uk/patterns

HOME & GARDEN

POLKA DOT PAN HOLDER

by Claire Garland

A stylish and practical kitchen accessory, this polka dot pan holder is
part sewn, part knitted and will cheer you as you cook.

YOU WILL NEED:

1 x 50g (1¾oz) ball grey
aran yarn – MC

Small amounts DK yarn for
the polka dots – CC

7mm (US size 10½) knitting needles

5.00mm (US size 8/H) crochet hook

Vintage fabric 22 x
22cm (8½ x 8½in)

Wool felt 20 x 20cm (8 x 8in)

*Tension: 15sts x 16.5 rows =
10cm in stocking stitch*

2 TO 3 HOURS

EASY

1. Pan holder

Md (make dot) – knit into front,
knit into back, knit into front of
next stitch (3sts yarn CC on RH
needle) turn, p3 tog, turn, k1.

In MC – Cast on 30sts.
Work st st for 4 rows.

Row 5: MC – k2, [CC – md, MC –
k5] 4 times, CC – md, MC – k3.
Cut yarn CC at end of row.
St st 5 rows.
Row 11: [MC – k5, CC – md] 4
times, CC – md, MC – k6.
St st 5 rows.
Rep last 12 rows (Rows 5 – 16) once.

Row 29: as row 5
End with 4 rows st st.
Cast off k-wise. Weave in all stray ends.

2. Attach yarn MC and CC held
together to one of the corners and work
16ch. Join with slip stitch in base of
first ch. Weave in ends. If necessary
lightly steam and re-shape into a
square, using the felt square as a guide.

3. Using the felt square as a guide
press a 1cm (⅜in) hem all round the
fabric square to wrong sides. Pin wrong
sides together, then whip stitch the
fabric to the knitted panel with the
felt square sandwiched between.

GROOVY RETRO WALLPAPER DECORATION

by Kirsty Neale

This three-dimensional hanging decoration is *so* 1970s. It's made from woodgrain-patterned paper and scraps of vintage wallpaper. Groovy!

YOU WILL NEED:

Woodgrain-patterned paper

Scraps of vintage wallpaper

PVA glue

Embroidery thread or yarn

Two wooden beads

2 HOURS

EASY

1. Copy the large template onto woodgrain paper and cut out six identical pieces. Repeat with the smaller template, cutting out six pieces of vintage wallpaper.

2. Fold all twelve pieces in half lengthways and press firmly along the fold to create a sharp crease. Stick each wallpaper piece over the centre of a woodgrain one to decorate.

3. Take two of the pieces and apply glue to the back of one, adding it just to the left side of the fold. Press the right-hand section of the second piece down on top, so the two pieces are half glued together, half free.

4. Now, apply glue to the left-hand side of the fold on the second piece. Press the right-hand section of a third piece down on top of it. Keep going, sticking all of the pieces together so they form a three-dimensional shape.

5. Fold a 50cm (20in) length of thread in half. Add a couple of beads, then knot the thread ends together. Place in the centre of the decoration, where all of the paper folds meet. Glue the first and last paper pieces together to hold the thread inside and finish your decoration.

Full-size templates for this project are available at: www.stitchcraftcreate.co.uk/patterns

1930s FLOWER GARLAND CUSHION

by Maggie Jones

This 1930s cushion has been made in colours echoing Clarice Cliff pottery and is worked in natural linen with felt flower shapes.

YOU WILL NEED:

Natural linen 30 x 30cm (12 x 12in)

Natural linen two pieces 30 x 16.5cm (12 x 6½in)

Felt: red, brown, dark green, mustard and peach

Tapestry wool in orange

Zip 24cm (9½in)

Threads to match linen and felt

Cushion pad 30cm (12in) square

Sewing machine (optional)

HALF A DAY

MEDIUM

1. To make the back, place right sides of the rectangular linen pieces together and sew 2.5cm (1in) together at each end of one long side for the zip placement. Press allowance open then insert the zip in the opening.

2. To make the front, use the templates to cut out the felt flower shapes in colours and shapes as shown

on the templates. Arrange them on the linen, in a circle shape as shown in the photograph, ensuring they are placed an equal distance from the centre of the fabric. Tack each flower down.

3. With matching sewing thread, use tiny stitches on the outside and inside of the flowers to stitch them to the linen.

4. With the tapestry wool, use chain stitch to accentuate the centre of the flowers.

5. Open the zip slightly. Place right sides of front and back together, and with 1cm (⅜in) seam allowance, sew all round the edge. Clip corners, turn right side out and press. Insert the pad to finish.

Full-size templates for this project are available at: www.stitchcraftcreate.co.uk/patterns

HOME & GARDEN

TECHNIQUES
CROCHET

Crochet abbreviations

Be aware that crochet terms in the US are different from those in the UK. This can be confusing as the same terms are used to refer to different stitches under each system. The list here gives abbreviations and a translation of US terms to UK terms.

UK term	US term
back loop single crochet (blsc)	back loop single crochet (blsc)
beginning (beg)	beginning (beg)
chain (ch)	chain (ch)
double crochet (dc)	single crochet (sc)
double treble (dtr)	treble crochet (tr)
half treble (htr)	half double crochet (hdc)
right side (RS)	right side (RS)
skip (sk)	skip (sk)
slip stitch (sl st)	slip(ped) stitch (sl st)
treble (tr)	double crochet (dc)
wrong side (WS)	wrong side (WS)

The starting loop or slipknot

Before you begin, you will need to make your first stitch. This will form the basis for all the following stitches. Make a loop near the cut end of the yarn and insert the crochet hook into the loop, picking up the end of the yarn leading to the ball. Draw this new loop of yarn through the existing loop, and gently pull on the cut end to tighten this new loop around the hook. This is your first stitch.

Chain

Abbreviation = ch

Almost all crochet items start with a length of chain stitches, and they also often appear within stitch patterns. Wherever the chain is required, it is made in the same way. To make a chain stitch, take the yarn over the hook, wrapping it from the back, up over the hook towards the front, and then down

and under the hook (every time the yarn is taken over the hook it should be done in this way). Now draw this new loop of yarn through the loop on the hook to complete the chain stitch.

Double crochet

Abbreviation = dc

A double crochet stitch is one of the most commonly used and easiest crochet stitches to make. To make a double crochet, start by inserting the hook into the work at the required point. Take the yarn over the hook and draw this new loop of yarn through the loop on the hook – there are now two loops on the hook. Take the yarn over the hook again and draw this new loop through both the loops on the hook. This completes the double crochet stitch.

1.

2.

Treble

Abbreviation = tr

This is the other most commonly used crochet stitch: while a double crochet stitch is a very short, compact stitch, a treble stitch is taller and will add more height to the work. To make a treble, wrap the yarn around the hook before inserting it into the work. Wrap the yarn around the hook again and draw this loop through the work – there are now three loops on the hook. Wrap the yarn around the hook once more and draw this new loop through just the first two loops on the hook – the original loop and this new loop. Wrap the yarn around the hook again and draw this new loop through both loops on the hook to complete the treble stitch.

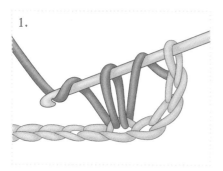

Half treble

Abbreviation = htr

A half treble stitch is a variation of a treble; its height is halfway between that of a double crochet and a treble stitch. To make a half treble, start in exactly the way a treble is made until there are three loops on the hook. Wrap the yarn around the hook once more and draw this new loop through all three loops on the hook to complete the half treble stitch.

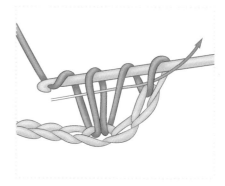

Slip stitch

Abbreviation = sl st

This stitch adds virtually no height to the work and is generally used either to move the hook and working loop to a new point, or to join pieces. To make a slip stitch, insert the hook into the work at the required point. Take the yarn over the hook and draw this new loop through both the work and the loop on the hook to complete the slip stitch.

KNITTING

Knitting abbreviations

Abbreviations are used in knitting patterns to shorten commonly used terms so that the instructions are easier to read and a manageable length. The following is a list of the abbreviations you need to make the projects in this book.

alt ....alternate
approx..........................approximately
Beg................................beginning
cm ....centimetre(s)
cont...............................continue
dec(s) ....decrease/decreasing
DK ....double knitting
dpns..............................double-pointed needles
foll................................following
g...................................gram(s)
g-st...............................garter stitch
inc................................increase(s)/increasing
in(s)..............................inch(es)
k ....knit
k2tog............................knit 2 stitches together
                             (1 stitch decreased)
k3tog............................knit 3 stitches together
                             (2 stitches decreased)
k2togtbl ....knit 2 stitches together
                             through back of loops
                             (1 stitch decreased)
kf&b.............................knit into front and back of
                             stitch (1 stitch increased)
m..................................make (e.g., m1)
mm ....millimetres
m1................................make one (increase 1 stitch)
n ....needle
oz.................................ounces
p ....purl
patt(s)...........................pattern(s)
pfb...............................purl into front and back of
                             stitch (to increase by 1 stitch)
p2tog............................purl 2 stitches together
                             (1 stitch decreased)
p3tog............................purl 3 stitches together
                             (2 stitches decreased)
pm................................place marker
psso ....pass slip stitch over

rem...............................remain/remaining
rep(s)............................repeat(s)
rnd ....round
RS................................right side
skpo.............................slip, knit, pass over
sl..................................slip
sl st ....slip stitch
ssk................................slip 2 stitches one at a time,
                             knit 2 slipped stitches together
                             (1 stitch decreased)
st st ....stockinette (stocking) stitch
                             (1 row k, 1 row p)
st(s)..............................stitch(es)
tbl................................through back of loop
tog ....together
WS ....wrong side
yd(s) ....yards(s)
yo.................................yarn over
* ....repeat directions following *
                             as many times as indicated or
                             to end of row
[ ]..................................instructions in square brackets
                             refer to larger sizes
( ) ....repeat instructions in round
                             brackets

Knitting terms

UK term	US term
stocking stitch	stockinette stitch
reverse stocking stitch	reverse stockinette stitch
moss stitch	seed stitch
double moss stitch or seed stitch	moss stitch
cast off	bind off
tension	gauge

Casting on

To begin knitting, you need to work a foundation row of stitches and this is called casting on. There are several ways to cast on stitches and a cable cast-on method is described here.

1. Take two needles and make a slip knot about 15cm (6in) from the end of the yarn on one needle. Hold this needle in your left hand. Insert the right-hand needle knitwise into the loop on the left-hand needle and wrap the yarn around the tip.

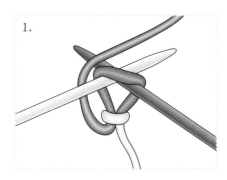

2. Pull the yarn through the loop to make a stitch but do not drop the stitch off the left-hand needle.

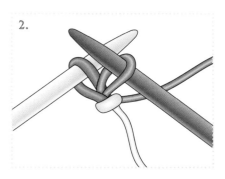

3. Slip the new stitch on to the left-hand needle by inserting the left-hand needle into the front of the loop from right to left. You will now have two stitches on the left-hand needle.

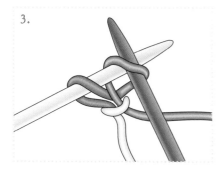

4. Insert the right-hand needle between the two stitches on the left-hand needle and wrap the yarn around the tip. Pull the yarn back through between the two stitches and place it on the left-hand needle, as in step 3. Repeat until you have cast on the required number of stitches.

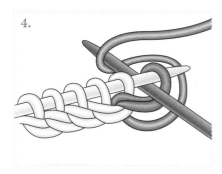

To cast on extra stitches mid row – work step 4 only, working the first stitch between the next two stitches already on the left-hand needle.

Using a stitch marker

Stitch markers are used to mark your place in a row of knitting and are especially useful in circular knitting, or knitting in the round, where it is not obvious where the circle begins and ends. They are usually made of plastic or metal and are slipped on to the knitting needle.

Knit stitch

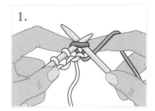 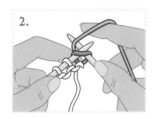  

Knit stitch (continental)

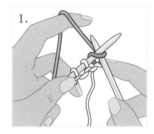 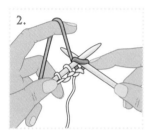 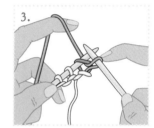 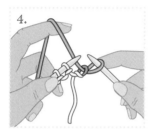

Purl stitch

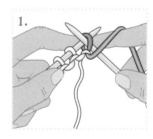  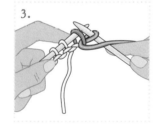 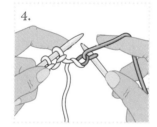

Purl stitch (continental)

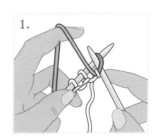 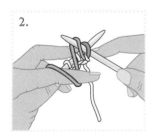 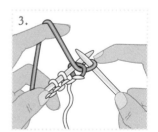 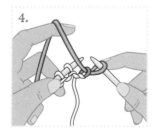

TECHNIQUES

Stockinette stitch (st st)

Stockinette or stocking stitch is formed by working alternate knit and purl rows. The knit rows are the right side of the fabric and the purl rows are the wrong side. Instructions for stockinette stitch in knitting patterns can be written as follows:

Row 1: RS Knit

Row 2: Purl

Or alternatively: work in st st (1 row k, 1 row p), beg with a k row.

Knitting in the round

Knitting in the round is a method where a tube of knitting is formed rather than a flat piece, so the knitting is worked in rounds, not rows. This can be done by using a circular needle or double-pointed needles. When you reach the end of a round you simply carry on knitting without turning the needles. Double-pointed needles are shorter than standard needles and are easier to handle than a circular needle when you only have a few stitches to work on or when working in the round.

1. Cast on normally, distributing the stitches evenly over three double-pointed needles.

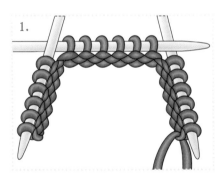

2. Continue knitting round, transferring the stitches along each needle so you have an equal number of stitches on each needle. You may want to place a stitch marker at the beginning of the round.

Changing yarn colour

1. Insert the tip of the right-hand needle into the next stitch, place the cut end of the new colour over the old colour and over the tip of the right-hand needle. Take the working end of the new colour and knit the next stitch, pulling the cut end off the needle over the working end as the stitch is formed so it is not knitted in. Hold the cut end down against the back of the work.

2. Once you've joined in all the colours that you need across the row, on the return row twist the yarns to join the blocks of colour together. When you change colour, always pick up the new colour from under the old yarn.

Increasing stitches

Increasing stitches is a way of shaping the knitting and there are several methods.

Make 1 (M1) – twist M1 to the left

This increase is used for shaping the thumb gusset on mitten gloves. Use both the right- and left-twisting versions for a neat finish to the gusset. The new stitch is made between two existing stitches using the horizontal thread that lies between the stitches.

1. Knit to the point where the increase is to be made. Insert the tip of the left-hand needle under the running thread from front to back.

2. Knit this loop through the back to twist it. By twisting it you prevent a hole appearing where the made stitch is.

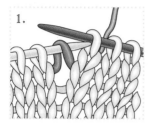

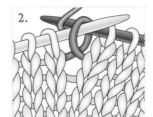

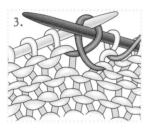

Make 1 (M1) – twist M1 to the right

1. Knit to the point where the increase is to be made. Insert the tip of the left-hand needle under the running thread from back to front.

2. Knit this loop through the front to twist it.

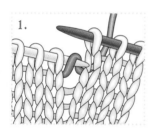

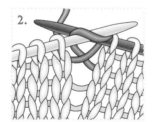

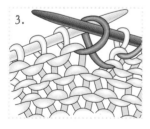

Knit into front and back (Kf&b)
An easy way to increase one stitch is by working into the front and back of the same stitch.

Knit into the front of the stitch. Do not slip the stitch off the left-hand needle but knit into it again through the back of the loop, then slip the original stitch off the left-hand needle. You can make a stitch on a purl row the same way but purling into the front and back of the stitch (pfb).

Decreasing stitches

As well as being able to increase stitches you will need to be able to decrease stitches for shaping. Stitches can be decreased singly or by several at once. Two methods are described here.

Decreasing one stitch –
knit 2 together (K2tog)
Knit to where the decrease is to be, insert the right-hand needle (as though to knit) through the next two stitches and knit them together as one stitch.

Decreasing one stitch –
purl 2 together (P2tog)
Purl to where the decrease is to be, insert the right-hand needle (as though to purl) through the next two stitches and purl them together as one stitch.

Casting off

Casting off (binding off) links and secures stitches together so that knitting cannot unravel when completed. Casting off is normally done following the stitch sequence, so a knit stitch is bound off knitwise and a purl stitch purlwise. Don't cast off too tightly as this may pull the fabric in. To bind off on a purl row, follow the Cast Off Knitwise steps but purl the stitches instead of knitting them.

Cast off knitwise

1. Knit the first two stitches. Insert the point of the left-hand needle into the front of the first stitch on the right-hand needle.

2. Lift the first stitch on the right-hand needle over the second stitch and off the needle. One stitch is left on the right-hand needle.

3. Knit the next stitch on the left-hand needle, so there are again two stitches on the right-hand needle. Lift the first stitch on the right-hand needle over the second stitch, as in step 2. Repeat this until one stitch is left on the right-hand needle. Cut the yarn (leaving a length long enough to sew in) and pass the end through the last stitch. Slip the stitch off the needle and pull the yarn end to tighten it.

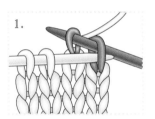

Darning in ends

Loose ends from casting on, binding off and changing colours can be woven into the knitting to secure them and create a neat look. Thread the loose end through a large-eyed tapestry or darning needle and pass the needle through the 'bumps' of the stitches on the back of the work for about 5cm (2in) and then snip off excess yarn.

Sewing up

There are different methods for seaming or sewing your knitted pieces together depending on the finish you want. If possible, sew up your items with the same yarn you used to knit them. If the yarn is very thick, highly textured or breaks easily, use a plain yarn in a matching colour.

Seaming with overcasting

Overcasting is a useful method of joining knitted pieces as it creates a narrow, flat seam. It is usually worked from the wrong side. Pin the pieces to be joined with their right sides together, matching the stitches exactly. Thread a tapestry or darning needle with yarn about 45cm (18in) long and join the yarn securely at the edge of the two seams. Work along the seam taking the needle under the strands at the edge of the seam, between the matched 'bumps', from back to front. Tighten the yarn gently over the knitted edge after each stitch, keeping the tension of each stitch the same.

Grafting

Grafting is used to join two pieces of knitting together. Working from right to left, insert a tapestry needle from the back of the work through the first stitch on each edge and pull the yarn through. Continue in this way, forming a new row of stitches.

I-cord

I-cord is a knitting technique used to create a knitted tube.

1. Cast on a small number of stitches on a circular or double-pointed needle. Push the stitches to the other end of the needle and turn the needle, so the first stitch you'll knit is the first one you cast on.

2. Knit the stitches, making sure you pull the yarn tight for the first stitch. Move the stitches to the other end of the needle. Repeat this process until the i-cord is the desired length.

SEWING

Basic Stitches

When sewing by hand choose a needle that matches the thickness of the thread you are using, so the thread passes easily through the fabric. All stitches can be started with a knot on the back of the work and finished off neatly at the back, usually with backstitch.

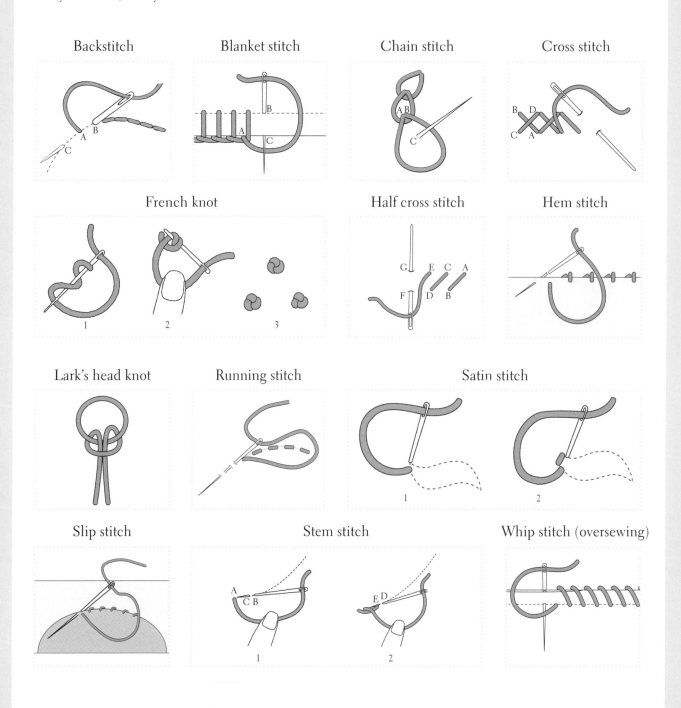

Backstitch

Blanket stitch

Chain stitch

Cross stitch

French knot

Half cross stitch

Hem stitch

Lark's head knot

Running stitch

Satin stitch

Slip stitch

Stem stitch

Whip stitch (oversewing)

CROSS STITCH CHARTS

Gentleman's Notebook

KEY

■ dark brown

Stitch count: 16H x 22W

New Home Card

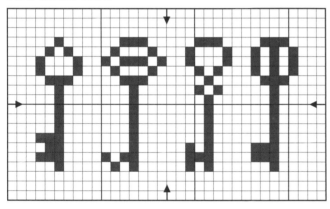

KEY

■ dark grey

Stitch count: 14H x 28W

Cute Vintage Coin Purse

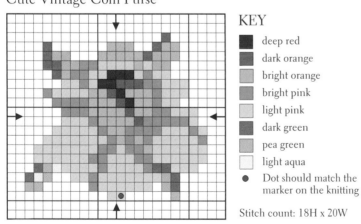

KEY

■ deep red
■ dark orange
■ bright orange
■ bright pink
■ light pink
■ dark green
■ pea green
□ light aqua
● Dot should match the
  marker on the knitting

Stitch count: 18H x 20W

Each coloured square represents a
cross stitch worked over a knitted stitch

All other templates for the projects
in this book can be found at
www.stitchcraftcreate.co.uk/patterns

CONTRIBUTORS

The publishers would like to thank all of the contributors
whose designs have been featured in this book:

Philippa Belcher- Love
www.facebook.com/pages/Piplotex/

Linda Bennett
www.bristolstvintage.com/

Daisy Bryan

Ruth Clemens
www.thepinkwhisk.co.uk

Linda Clements

Laurel Deville

Anna Fazakerley
www.twobirdscraft.com/

Angela Finch

Penny Fitzmaurice

Mary Fogg

Lisa Fordham

Claire Garland
www.claire-garland.blogspot.co.uk/

Chloë Haywood
www.Hatastic.co.uk

Jeni Hennah

Samantha Horn

Lauren Howden

Maggie Jones
www.facebook.com/CraftDemon

Sarah Joyce

Ellen Kharade

Julia Liddell

Tirke Linnemann

Danielle Lowy
www.rubbishrevamped.org.uk

Annie Marston
www.nimblefingersandsteadyeyebrows.blogspot.co.uk

Jacky Massos

Sof McVeigh
www.thehomemadecompany.com

Elsie Molyneux
www.elsiemoflowers.com

Lucy Morris
www.prettyvintage.co.uk/

Kirsty Neale
www.kirstyneale.typepad.com/

Sarah Oatley
www.DrawnThreads.co.uk
Drawnthreads.uk@googlemail.com

Lotte Oldfield
www.lotteoldfield.com/

Laura Pashby James
www.nimblefingersandsteadyeyebrows.blogspot.co.uk

Fiona Pearce

Fiona-Grace Peppler

Louise Scott

Lynsey Searle

Selina Steffen

Amanda Stinton
www.sewimadethis.blogspot.co.uk/

Shenna Swan

Sue Trevor

Eloise Varin
www.facebook.com/Eloisevintagecrations

Anna Wilson

Benjamin Wilson

Lauraine Wishart
www.mobilecrafts.co.uk

Many of the materials used to make
the projects in this book can be found
at: www.stitchcraftcreate.co.uk.

INDEX

A DAVID & CHARLES BOOK
© F&W Media International, Ltd 2013

David & Charles is an imprint of F&W Media International, Ltd
Brunel House, Forde Close, Newton Abbot, TQ12 4PU, UK

F&W Media International, Ltd is a subsidiary of F+W Media, Inc
10151 Carver Road, Suite #200, Blue Ash, OH 45242, USA

Text and Designs © F&W Media International, Ltd 2013
Layout and Photography © F&W Media International, Ltd 2013

First published in the UK and USA in 2013

A catalogue record for this book is available from the British Library.

ISBN-13: 978-1-4463-0372-6 paperback
ISBN-10: 1-4463-0372-1 paperback

Printed in China by RR Donnelley for:
F&W Media International, Ltd
Brunel House, Forde Close, Newton Abbot, TQ12 4PU, UK

10 9 8 7 6 5 4 3 2 1

Publisher: Alison Myer
Junior Acquisitions Editor: Verity Graves-Morris
Desk Editor: Hannah Kelly
Project Editor: Jane Trollope
Proofreader: Linda Clements
Senior Designer: Victoria Marks
Photographer: Sian Irvine
Senior Production Controller: Kelly Smith

F+W Media publishes high quality books on a wide range of subjects.
For more great book ideas visit: www.stitchcraftcreate.co.uk